Stealth Technology
The Art of Black Magic

J. Jones, edited by Matt Thurber

AERO
A division of TAB BOOKS
Blue Ridge Summit, PA

FIRST EDITION
THIRD PRINTING

Copyright © 1989 by TAB BOOKS
Printed in the United States of America

Library of Congress Cataloging in Publication Data

Joseph, J. (Joseph)
    Stealth technology : the art of black magic / by J. Jones : edited
by Matt Thurber.
        p.   cm.
    Includes index.
    ISBN 0-8306-8281-3   ISBN 0-8306-8381-X (pbk.)
    1. Stealth aircraft—United States. I. Thurber, Matt.
    II. Title.
    UG1243.J66 1989   88-35709
    358.4′183—dc19   CIP

TAB BOOKS offers software for sale. For information and a catalog, please contact
TAB Software Department, Blue Ridge Summit, PA 17294-0850.

Questions regarding the content of this book should be addressed to:

    Reader Inquiry Branch
    TAB BOOKS
    Blue Ridge Summit, PA 17294-0214

Edited by Suzanne L. Cheatle

Front cover illustration by Larry Selman; backcover photograph courtesy of U.S. Air Force.

Contents

Acknowledgments

I would like to give my most sincere thanks to the following military services and aerospace corporations for providing photographs in this book: Aerospatiale, Bell Helicopter TEXTRON, Bell Aerospace, Boeing Helicopters, California Microwave Inc., General Dynamics Corporation, Goodyear, Lockheed-Austin Division, Lockheed-California Company, Lockheed Missiles & Space Company, McDonnell Douglas-St. Louis, McDonnell Douglas Helicopters, Northrop Corporation, Rockwell International, Royal Norwegian Air Force, Royal Swedish Air Force, Schweizer Aircraft, Sikorsky Aircraft (United Technologies), U.S. Air Force, U.S. Department of Defense, and U.S. Navy.

I also wish to thank my publisher and the editorial staff at TAB BOOKS for their valuable assistance in helping me complete this book about stealth technology: Raymond A. Collins, Vice President, Editorial; Robert E. Ostrander, Executive Editor; Jeff Worsinger, Aviation Acquisitions Editor; Suzanne L. Cheatle, Coordinator of Outside Editing; Teresa Dingle, Editorial Assistant.

I also want to thank the following individuals for their assistance with text and photographs/artwork: Erik Simonsen, Public Relations at Rockwell International, is also a freelance writer/photographer. His work has appeared in numerous issues of Combat Arms International, and his photographs have appeared in countless other publications. Wayne Atkinson provided his assistance in preparing some of the photographs that appear in this book. Matt Thurber provided his time and effort in helping prepare the final manuscript.

Introduction

Stealth. The word conjures images of fighter jets and bombers sneaking into enemy territory, jinking around obstacles while hugging the earth to avoid detection by batteries of radars and eagle-eyed sentinels.

The word also raises many questions, for the application of stealth technology to military programs conforms beautifully to the meaning of the word. In the same way that *stealth* means the act of proceeding furtively, secretly, or imperceptibly, the American military's application of stealth technology has proceeded so furtively, secretly, and imperceptibly that few hard facts about the subject are known by the public.

Information about stealth is available, however, to those who diligently search for it. After years of research, I have been able to apply my knowledge of existing technology and new developments to the skimpy facts that have been released about military stealth programs. The result is the up-to-date information in this book, which will enable you to learn more about what makes stealth technology tick and how this technology is applied to military aircraft.

The first half of this book covers the technology used to make a stealth aircraft nearly invisible to enemy radars and infrared detectors, as well as make them difficult to hear or see by humans. These techniques are commonly and collectively referred to as the application of *low-observable*, or stealth, technology. In the rest of the book, I've described the manned and unmanned aircraft that employ stealth technology and listed their specifications and capabilities. One section includes some incidents these aircraft have been involved in, such as the crash of a Lockheed F-117A stealth fighter north of Bakersfield, California, in 1986, and a reported case of a U.S. stealth aircraft successfully penetrating Soviet airspace without being detected.

Although a few details about stealth aircraft have become public, chances are that most stealth programs will remain under tight security for many years to come. An exception to this is the Northrop B-2A stealth bomber, of which the U.S. Air Force released what it calls an accurate artist's conception in early 1988 and photographs in late 1988. The Air Force, in fact, invited dignitaries and the press to the rollout of the B-2 on November 22, 1988. Also in 1988, the Air Force released a photograph of the supersecret F-117A fighter.

This could be evidence that the Air Force is relaxing its stance on releasing hard information on stealth programs in an effort to ensure continued funding, or it could simply be an admission that stealth technology is going to be part of every aircraft or aerospace weapon that rolls off the assembly line during the rest of this century.

Stealth technology is not restricted to aircraft. It might find its way into many types of military vehicles. On May 25, 1988, Defense Secretary Frank Carlucci said that the U.S. Navy is studying the possibility of applying stealth technology to warships as a means of countering long-range cruise missiles. Clearly, stealth is here to stay and will find widespread application in a variety of military programs.

Stealth technology represents a pure application of state-of-the-art scientific discoveries to conceal aircraft by deceiving or eliminating enemy detection capability. For the casual observer, stealth might seem to be more black magic courtesy of the U.S. Department of Defense, but remember, unlike comic-book dreams of invisibility, stealth is simply applied science. There is nothing mysterious or magical about it, as you will see in the following pages.

—J. Jones

Chapter One

Stealth in the Past

STEALTH IS NOT A NEW IDEA; IT IS SIMPLY A NEW NAME FOR SOMETHING that has been going on for eons. Nature has put its own form of stealth technology to use by, for example, coloring insects and animals so that they blend into their backgrounds. Humans learned to use stealth, probably by observing nature, and have been using it in various forms for years—the most basic being camouflage and decoying. These two methods are still in use today, and the reason they are used is also the reason so much money is being poured into stealth research, not only by the United States, but also many other countries as well: to prevent rival armies from detecting each other or gaining knowledge of the purpose of each other's missions.

Modern stealth technology fulfills that basic goal by putting to use techniques far more advanced than camouflage and decoying, although those methods are still used as an inexpensive first step in most military stealth programs. The development of stealth technology beyond the camouflage stage didn't occur until airplanes became tools of war, although some thought had been given to the subject prior to World War I.

In the early 1900s, Germany built some airplanes with transparent wing, fuselage, and empennage coverings. An Austro-Hungarian air service officer, Lt. Eduard Nittner, flew an Etrich Taube monoplane in May and June 1912, whose airframe was covered with a transparent material called *emaillit*. According to historical sources, when the Taube flew at 900 feet and above it could not be seen by observers on the ground. When the Taube flew at 700 feet above the ground, the observers said that the internal framework of the Taube's airframe was "faintly visible." Emaillit was derived from celluloid, and in liquid form it is known as *emaillit fabric dope*.

Cellon was another transparent material. It was applied by the Germans to several aircraft used during World War I without a great amount of success.

In 1935, the Soviets experimented with a transparent material called *rodoid*. It was applied over the airframe of a Yakovlev AIR-4 airplane; and the airplane's internal structure was painted a silvery white color to make it harder to see. The project met with little success, although at times ground observers failed to spot the airplane even though they could hear it. From a distance of a few hundred feet, however, the observers could easily see the airplane's white framework through its transparent skin.

Another German stealth project resulted from the advent of radar during World War II. This was probably the first attempt to develop new stealth technology to hide a military craft from radar. It represented a departure from earlier, which efforts that were focused on reducing a craft's *visual signature* (the ease with which it could be detected visually).

The Germans applied several coats of a radar-absorbing material to the snorkels of some of their U-boats (submarines). This was done so that radar-equipped Allied airplanes would not be able to detect the U-boats when crews needed to poke the snorkels above the surface to look around. In later years, this project would be called an attempt to reduce the radar signature of the snorkel. For some reason, the Germans didn't apply this radar-absorbent material to the U-boat's hull or to any airplanes.

In the United States during World War II, however, application of stealth technology was initiated primarily to reduce airplanes' chances of being detected by radar. One radar-absorbent coating material was developed by Northrop around 1945 and was known as MX-410. It was somewhat effective, but too many coats added too much weight to the airplane and adversely affected its performance. In some instances, the MX-410 coating made the airplane too heavy to fly.

Not much is known about subsequent stealth developments, primarily because the U.S. government considers the subject highly classified. As technology blossomed following World War II, research and development continued into stealth technology, but it wasn't until the U.S. government publicly admitted in 1980 that it even had a stealth program that any substantial information about stealth started to become available.

Chapter Two

The Government Stealth Press Conference

ON AUGUST 22, 1980, THE U.S. GOVERNMENT HELD A PRESS CONFERENCE at the Pentagon where, for the first time, the existence of an American stealth program was officially disclosed. The conference was given by then Secretary of Defense Harold Brown, Undersecretary of Defense for Research and Engineering William Perry, and the Air Force's Deputy Chief of Staff for Research and Development Lt. Gen. Kelly Burke.

Brown spoke first.

Brown: I am announcing today a major technological advance of great military significance.

This so-called stealth technology enables the United States to build manned and unmanned aircraft that cannot be successfully intercepted with existing air defense systems. We have demonstrated to our satisfaction that the technology works.

This achievement will be a formidable instrument of peace. It promises to add unique dimension to our tactical forces and to be the deterrent strength of our strategic forces. At the same time, it will provide us capabilities that are wholly consistent with our pursuit of verifiable arms control agreements, in particular with the provisions of SALT II.

For three years we've successfully maintained the security of this program. This is because of the conscientious efforts of the relatively few people in the executive branch and legislative branch who were briefed on the activity and the contractors working on it.

However, in the last few months, the circle of people knowledgeable about the program has widened, partly because of the increased size of the effort, and partly because of the debate underway in the Congress on new bomber proposals. Regrettably, there have been several leaks about the stealth program during the last few days, actually the last couple of weeks, in the press and there's been television news coverage.

In the face of these leaks, I believe that it's not appropriate or credible for us to deny the existence of this program. And it is now important to correct some of the leaked information that misrepresented the Administration's position on a new bomber program. The so-called stealth bomber was not a factor in our decision in 1977 to cancel the B-1; indeed, the so-called stealth bomber was not then yet in design. There were plenty of other good reasons to cancel the B-1, and I've been through those many times.

I am gratified that, as yet, none of the most sensitive and significant classified information about the characteristics of this program has been disclosed. An important objective of the announcement today is to make clear the kinds of information that we intend scrupulously to protect at the highest security level. Dr. Perry, a chief architect of this program, will elaborate on this point further.

In sum, we've developed a new technology of extraordinary military significance. We are vigorously applying this technology to develop a number of military aircraft, and these programs are showing very great promise.

We can take tremendous pride in this latest achievement of American technology. It can play a major role in the strengthening of our strategic and tactical forces without in any way endangering any of our arms-control initiatives. And it can contribute to the maintenance of peace by posing a new and significant offset to the Soviet Union's attempt to gain military ascendancy by weight of numbers.

(Brown introduces Dr. Perry.)

Perry: World War II demonstrated the decisive role that air power can play in military operations. It also demonstrated the potential of radar as a primary means of detecting aircraft and directing fire against them. On balance, though, the advantage clearly was with the aircraft. Subsequent to World War II, both ground-launched and air-launched defensive missiles were developed and most significantly, they were married with radar fire-control systems. This substantially increased the effectiveness of air-defense systems intended to shift the balance against the aircraft. For the last few decades, we have been working on techniques to defeat radar-controlled air-defense systems. Presently, our military aircraft make substantial use of electronic countermeasures [ECMs], popularly known as *jamming*, which tends to degrade the effectiveness of these radars. By these means we have maintained the effectiveness of our military aircraft in the face of very formidable and very effective radar-directed defensive missiles.

However, the Soviets continue to place very heavy emphasis on the development and deployment of air-defense missiles in an attempt to offset the advantage which we have in air power. They have built thousands of surface-to-air missile [SAMs] launchers. They employ radars with very high power and with a tracking technique which is known as *monopulse*, both of which tend to make electronic countermeasures very difficult to employ. And in just the last few years they have developed air-to-air missiles [AAMs] which are guided by what we call *look-down radars*, and these are radars that have special tracking circuits which allow them to track an aircraft flying low to the ground—that is, an aircraft which is flying in the so-called ground clutter.

Because of these developments and because of the importance we attach to maintaining our air superiority, we have for years been developing what we call *penetration technology:* the technology that degrades the effectiveness of radars and other sensors that are used by air-defense systems. A particular emphasis has been placed on developing that technology which makes an aircraft invisible to radar. In the early sixties, we applied a particular version of this technology to some of our reconnaissance aircraft. And again in the seventies we applied it to cruise missiles then being developed both for the Tomahawk and ALCM (air-launched cruise missile).

By the summer of 1977, it became clear that this technology could be considerably extended in its effectiveness and could be applied to a wide class of aircraft, including manned aircraft. We concluded that it was possible to build aircraft so difficult to detect that they could not be successfully engaged by any existing air-defense systems. Recognizing the great significance of such a development, we took three related actions: first of all, we made a tenfold increase in the investment which we are making in this penetration technology, the underlying technology which allows us to defeat the radar systems. Secondly, we initiated a number of very high priority development programs with a purpose of applying this technology. And finally, we gave the entire program extraordinary security protection, even to the point of classifying the very existence of the program.

Initially, we were able to limit knowledge of the program to a very few government officials in both the executive and legislative branches, and indeed succeeded in maintaining complete secrecy about the program. But, as the program increased in size—and its current annual funding is perhaps 100-fold greater that it was at the initiation of the program—it did become necessary to include more people in the knowledge of the program. But today the existence of a stealth program has become public knowledge.

But even as we acknowledge the existence of a stealth program, we will be drawing a new security line to protect that information about the program which could facilitate Soviet countermeasures. We will continue to protect at the highest level information of the following nature: first of all, the specific techniques which we employ to reduce detectability; secondly, the specific degree of success we have achieved with each of these techniques; thirdly, the characteristics of specific vehicles being developed; fourthly, funds being applied to specific programs; and finally, the schedules or the operational dates which go with these specific programs.

With these ground rules, I think you can see that I am extremely limited in what I can tell you about the program. I will volunteer this much. First of all, stealth technology does not involve a single technical approach—a single gimmick, so to speak—but is rather a complex synthesis of many. Even if I were willing to describe to you how we do this, I could not do so in a sentence or even in a paragraph. Secondly, while we have made remarkable progress in this technology in the last three years, we have been building on the excellent work done in our defense technology program over the last two decades. Thirdly, this technology—theoretically at least—could be applied to any military vehicle which can be attacked by radar-directed fire. In our studies, we are considering all such applications and are moving with some speed to develop those particular applications, which on the one hand are the most practical and on the other hand which have the greatest military significance. Finally, I can tell you that, that has included flight tests of a number of different vehicles.

Questions from the assembled media representatives followed:

Question: Can these technologies also defeat other means of detection, such as infrared and so on?

Brown: The general description of stealth technology includes ideas and designs that are directed also at reducing detectability by other means. Radar is the means that is best able to detect and intercept aircraft now. It's no accident that the systems that exist are radar systems. But stealth technology extends beyond radar. Bill [Perry], do you want to add anything there?

Perry: That is correct.

Question: I ask because you mention other vehicles, and I wonder if you're getting ready to have a complete turnover in the whole military inventory—tanks and all the rest.

Brown: It's a little too early to say that. I think what Bill was trying to say was that stealth technology is applicable against anything that is detected and attacked through detection by radar. But how practical it is for various kinds of vehicles is another matter.

Question: Gentlemen, you refer here to its effectiveness against existing air-defense systems. How about the kind of air-defense systems which the Russians seem to be moving toward in the year 1990?

Brown: Those are the ones that we are talking about. The ones that are now in development and could be deployed during the rest of this decade are the kinds of detection systems that we believe that this will be able to render ineffective. It will always be the case that whenever there is a major new development of military technology—a measure, let's call it—there will be countermeasures and there will be counter-countermeasures. We've been looking at both of those. Our judgment is that the balance is strongly tilted in the direction of penetration by this technology and that there will be later fluctuations around that new equilibrium point.

Question: Is there any sign that the Soviets might be able to catch up and match this technology for penetrating themselves?

Brown: It depends on how much they do and how fast they are able to do it. We are not aware of any comparable effort in the Soviet Union. But of course, the Soviets are the ones who have spent tens of billions, probably over 100 billion dollars, on air defense. And this favors penetration over air defense. A Soviet development of this kind would also make our air defenses less capable, except to the extent that we would be ahead on countermeasures, but we haven't expended nearly as much on air defense. Bill [Perry], do you want to add to this?

Perry: That's correct.

Question: Is this applicable to existing vehicles, existing aircraft?

Brown: These are new designs.

Question: You'd have to build new things to take advantage . . .

Brown: These are new designs.

Question: I'm puzzled by your comments about how secret this is. If this was such a secret technology, why was the possibility of a bomber with lower radar cross-section alluded to in the arms control impact statements in 1980, in [President] Carter's Georgia Tech speech and in your own posture statement?

Brown: Well, we have tried to reduce radar cross-sections. That is hardly a revolutionary new idea, and indeed successive generations of aircraft have had lower cross-sections. Indeed, the air-launch cruise missile has a lower radar cross-section than the B-1 bomber by a factor of what? One-hundred. So that's not a new idea. The new idea is how to reduce it still further and how far you can reduce it.

Question: What about the stories written in March 1979 about an invisible bomber based on the arms control impact statement? In other words, it seems like it wasn't a secret a year ago.

Brown: Then why are you all here?

Question: When are we likely to see this invisible bomber? How far down the pike is it?

Brown: Well, there have been flight tests, as Bill [Perry] said. We also do not intend to make the details of the program, including the appearance of the vehicles, public.

Question: What kind of ball park are you talking about? Are we talking a decade . . . ?

Brown: It's hard to believe that you can have things operational for very long and not let some things get out, but we're going to try to keep that kind of detail secret as long as we possibly can.

Question: On Sunday last week, you said the Administration does not have a plan to build a manned bomber.

Brown: That's not what I said. What I was asked was—and I was there so I know what I said. What I was asked was, "Will there be a decision on building a new bomber before the election?" My answer was, "There will not be a decision on building a new bomber this year." We have a number of advanced designs in the design stage based on various kinds of technologies, including this one. The authorization bill for the fiscal '81 defense appropriation bill, which is now in the final stages of adoption, and the report that accompanies it from the conference committee calls on the Defense Department to evaluate for use as a multipurpose follow-on bomber the B-1 modifications, FB-111 modifications, and advanced technology, and to decide by March 31st. That's compatible with our design studies, the status of our design studies.

Question: (Inaudible.)

Brown: Well, it's in the design stage, and I would judge that we could be able to evaluate it by roughly that time next year. Again, let me defer to Kelly and Bill on that.

Burke: Yes, that evaluation schedule is compatible with, I believe, it is March 15th, rather than March 31st.

Question: Could you tell us whether there have been operational flights in reconnaissance aircraft using stealth technology?

Brown: No, I will not comment on operational matters or on the stage of development.

Question: It's been the suggestion that the Administration is releasing news of the stealth bomber now in order to answer charges by Presidential Candidate Reagan that the B-1 bomber is one example of how the Administration has been soft on defense. Now how would you answer that? How would you answer Reagan?

Brown: First, I would repeat what I said, which is that the decision on the B-1 was not based on the possibility of a stealth bomber because that was not then even in the design stage. As to how good an answer this major breakthrough is to such charges, I will leave that to you to judge. But as to its purpose, I want to be quite clear. That was not the purpose of our action at this time. We would much preferred to have kept this secret for a longer time, as long as we could. But given the expansion of the circle of people who knew, which was inevitable because of the increase in size of the program and the involvement of additional congressional people—Congress, after all, does have a constitutional responsibility to appropriate funds—I suppose that it was inevitable that leaks would occur.

It was only after leaks had occurred to at least one magazine, one newspaper, and at least one television network, that it became clear that the existence of the program could no longer be kept secret. It was only then that we decided that it was necessary to say as much as we said—to draw a new line beyond which we would not be prepared to go.

Question: You are saying this is not a political reaction to Ronald Reagan, coming out here today and . . .

Brown: No, not at all. This is a reaction to the fact that the public knows, as a result of these leaks, that there is such a program. And it is important that we clarify some things and draw a new line.

Question: What do you think of the way Reagan's been reacting to our defense structure? I mean, using the ships story the other day and the charges about being soft on defense. Do you think he is being irresponsible?

Brown: That is a separate question. I have and will continue to try to avoid partisan characterizations. I believe that the Administration's defense program has been sensible. By moving to increase our military capabilities steadily and significantly and continuously, we are responding properly to the kinds of military threats we might face. I think it is a serious matter when individuals claim that the United States is very weak. When it is claimed that the Soviets greatly surpass us in all categories, I think that is incorrect and I think it undermines our security by emboldening our potential adversaries, dispiriting our allies, and misleading the American people. But you know, I'm not the one who has connected that with this program.

Question: Back to the aircraft. With the progress that you have made in penetration technology, has that led you and other senior defense officials to decide that the conventional bomber system—B-1 variance, stretched FB-111—are no longer the right way to go? Any new bomber will probably be built with this new technology.

Brown: The relative capabilities of existing and new technologies are part of the study in the case of the bombers that we will be doing. This certainly is a big factor, but I have not prejudged the outcome. Bill [Perry], what would you say?

Perry: The negative judgment which we made about the B-1 in 1977 we made without the benefit of a design study underway for the stealth bomber. It was just based on the relative ineffectiveness of the B-1 in penetrating Soviet air defenses, not in comparison with any other potential bomber.

Question: Does it make any sense to build a plane . . .

Brown: Let's come back to the Burt question. We haven't responded. What he is saying is, "In the 1990s, will there be anything but stealth aircraft?" and I think the answer is "Yes, there will." Because, you know, there are various features for aircraft. The ability to detect the aircraft is a very important one, but there are other features of aircraft that also determine how capable they are. Kelly [Burke], do you want to comment on that?

Burke: Well, that's right, and of course, you can only prioritize one design goal at a time, and obviously you don't get any desirable feature without giving up some other desirable features.

Question: Have there been any new scientific breakthroughs brought to bear on this? Has there been any new scientific principle, any breakthrough as you might say?

Brown: These are technological. There is no new fundamental law of science involved.

Question: General Kelly, I was wondering what your personal view was. There is a deadline in the Congressional mandate in the authorization bill, as you know, for a bomber to be flying in 1987. Would you be willing to gamble on stealth being ready by then, or would you like a stop-gap airplane, or do you think maybe that deadline should be extended to see how stealth works out? What is your personal view on that?

Burke: That it's premature to try and answer that. Along with Rick's question, those are the explicit questions that we are seeking to answer in the recommendations we make to the Congress on the 15th of March, and there is an enormous amount of work to be done between now and then—not just quantitative analysis, but a lot of engineering evaluation.

Brown: It's too soon to say what the precise mix of our capabilities in the 1990s will be, but it is not too soon to say that by making existing air-defense systems essentially ineffective, this alters the military balance significantly.

Question: Is Lockheed involved in this program, specifically, the Lockheed Skunkworks?

Brown: We have decided we are not going to reveal the names of any of the contractors because if we did, that would allow attempts to find out about this, to focus in on one or a few places.

Question: You said that it was new technology. Does this mean that it is not retrofittable to existing aircraft? And if it requires a new generation of aircraft, how expensive a new generation of aircraft?

Brown: Bill [Perry], why don't you answer this? I think I answered the first part before.

Perry: I mentioned that this is a complex synthesis of many technologies. Some of them may be applicable to modifying existing aircraft. In their entirety, they are not applicable. They require a design from the ground up. The cost of airplanes built with this combination of technologies on a dollar-per-pound basis is probably not substantially different from the cost of building airplanes on a dollar-per-pound basis with conventional techniques.

Question: With its potential, what would you guess might the percentage be of aircraft that we have of this sort . . . ?

Brown: I have a guess, but I don't think I'll give it. I think it is so speculative it doesn't make sense to do that.

Question: . . . *Unmanned vehicle,* are you referring to the cruise missile?

Brown: Well, any unmanned aerodynamic vehicle I guess you can describe as a cruise missile. But you know . . .

Perry: Cruise missiles and drones.

Brown: Yes. But, you know, cruise missiles and drones share characteristics.

Question: Dr. Perry, you have said publicly that you will recommend to the gentleman on your left several hundred million dollars in the next budget for development of a penetrating bomber so that by 1985 you could decide whether it could go into production for 1988 and IOC [initial operational capability]. On the assumption that you will still make such a recommendation, will it involve the technologies being discussed here today?

Perry: I'm not prepared to come to that conclusion yet.

Question: What conclusion, sir?

Brown: That it will.

Perry: I'm not prepared to come to any conclusion about what I will recommend until next spring. This is when the recommendation will be made. And I'm still studying it, as is General Burke, as he indicated.

Question: You are no longer saying you will recommend inclusion of penetrating-bomber development in the next budget?

Perry: No. I'm saying that I have not determined yet whether that recommendation would be for a stealth bomber or some other design. That is still being considered.

Brown: Well, the next budget is 1982, and that is being formulated now.

Question: That is exactly the one Dr. Perry has spoken about publicly. Do we infer from your answer that you may recommend a bomber that is not a stealth type—that it could happen?

Perry: I think you could infer from it that I still have an open mind on the question.

Question: Why would you recommend any other kind of a bomber for the out-years than a stealth type?

Brown: You know, we have said several times that ability to penetrate is only one, albeit a major, characteristic of a new generation of aircraft. I think you have to look at all the characteristics—you know, range, payload, and everything else. I hope that we have left the impression, the proper impression, the one that I believe, that this is a very important characteristic. But I don't think that we should now draw a conclusion that we don't have to draw until next spring.

Question: Dr. Brown, you just said, though, that any system like this that can wipe out existing air defense alters the military balance in a significant way.

Brown: It sure does.

Question: All right. But if you're not going to penetrate with it, what difference does it make?

Brown: The potential already has the effect. But you know, this is a major advantage to such a system, but we're not going to make a decision now. We can just let you know what our impressions are, and I think we've made our impressions clear.

Question: No, but are you suggesting, though, that despite the great advance you've made in this particular area, it might turn out that you can't apply it to a bomber system because it disturbs other necessary advantages of . . .

Brown: Yes. I'm sure you can apply it to a bomber system. I don't want to judge the overall characteristics of a design that's still in process. And you know that, I think, is the proper attitude and it is the attitude I take. From what I've said and from your own reactions, it's clear that a design with this technology and this capability to penetrate has a big advantage going for it.

Question: How about fighters? Will it apply to fighter technology?

Brown: The same thing applies to fighters. I think you can apply this technology across the board. Bill [Perry]? Do you want to be more specific?

Question: When you say all military vehicles, do you mean everything from ICBMs [inter-continental ballistic missiles] to tanks, to ships, to everything?

Perry: In principle, it could be applied to any of them.

Brown: It dosen't help some as much as others.

Perry: It is our ability of applying it. The difference it would make in military effectiveness may be dramatically different from vehicle to vehicle. The cost of applying it may be different.

Brown: Some vehicles aren't primarily detected by radar. They are detected by eyeball.

Question: Is the answer on whether a new bomber might be built that could not penetrate, and I do take that from the answer that that is conceivable . . .

Brown: No.

Question: Is it conceivable?

Brown: If we were sure it wouldn't penetrate, if we had real doubts about its penetration capability, we would cancel it just as we canceled the B-1.

Question: I didn't mean that. That would not have that technology. There would not be the stealth technology.

Brown: I think any new bomber will use some elements of this technology. There is just no doubt about that in my mind.

Question: One of the published reports said that three of these test vehicles crashed because of unorthodox configuration.

Brown: Bill [Perry], do you want to comment on that?

Perry: The report is incorrect.

Question: There were two crashes?

Brown: The report was incorrect, and the report was allegedly that they crashed, that there were crashes because of the unorthodox design.

Question: Let's rephrase it then. Have any of your invisible airplanes crashed?

Brown: We're not going to talk about the test program. I think all of you have watched more visible test programs, have seen what happens in a test program.

Question: Dr. Brown, do you personally believe that we need a new bomber of some kind for the eighties or nineties, or is that still an open question in your mind?

Brown: I continue to have an open mind on that. I am sure that we will continue to need to be able to have an air-breathing component of our deterrent force. We have plans and we will have forces that do that, using the cruise missile launched from B-52s, using penetrating bombers, penetrating B-52s, through the mid- and probably the late eighties. Beyond that, whether we need a purely penetrating component is an open question in my mind.

Question: How do you expect the Soviets to react to this, and do you think it will have any effect on arms-control talks?

Brown: I've spoken to the latter question in my statement. If you believe that a Soviet capability to shoot down all aerodynamic aircraft of the U.S. is a good thing, then you should be very against this development. If you believe that a U.S. capability to penetrate Soviet air defense contributes to deterrence as I do, then you will regard this as an advance in stabilizing the arms competition. There is no doubt that bombers which have a longer reaction time are not the destabilizing component. That's land-based fixed ICBMs.

With respect to arms control, these like any other aircraft—if they are intercontinental aircraft, intercontinental bombers, heavy bombers—would be included in that part of the agreement. If they are tactical aircraft, then they would be included in any, not SALT, but some other arms-control agreement that covered those.

The Soviets, I am sure as a result, not of this revelation, but as a result of the leaks over previous weeks, are already, I'm sure, looking very hard at this technology and scratching their heads hard and will go to work hard on countermeasures, as you would expect. Because the Soviets have put so much more into air defense and have concentrated on large numbers much more than we, I think this benefits the U.S. and the military balance.

Question: Dr. Brown, it seems to me if you have an invisible bomber, then that could become a first-strike weapon.

Brown: I don't understand. You mean ability to penetrate air defenses makes something . . .

Question: They can't see it.

Question: If they can't see or hear you coming . . .

Question: It would give you a little surprise. (Laughter.)

Brown: The ability to penetrate air defenses is not a first-strike capability. The ability to penetrate air defenses is a good retaliatory capability. Bombers are not the instrument of choice in a surprise attack. There is just no question about that.

Question: With this invisible bomber, you couldn't just take off and bomb a target without anybody knowing you were coming?

Brown: They would know, but too late to intercept you. But not too late to retaliate.

Perry: Or—I do want to emphasize the point, though—that the term *invisible* is strictly a figure of speech. It is not an invisible airplane. In the strict sense of the word, it is not invisible. You can see it. And it is also not invisible to radar. It can be seen by radars if you get the airplane close enough to the radars.

Brown: But too late to engage in air defense. But not too late to retaliate.

Question: Is this an evolving technology? Are you going to be better at it in two years or five years?

Brown: Yes.

That's it. Thank you very much.

The press conference was over.

Chapter Three

Low-Observable Techniques

A VARIETY OF TECHNIQUES ARE USED WHEN APPLYING STEALTH TECH-nology to military vehicles. Although most of these techniques are familiar to aircraft designers, until recently the materials and methods needed to put the technology to use had not been perfected. Now computer-aided design (CAD) and advanced composite materials are making possible great strides in the application of stealth technology. As exploration into the manufacture of new composite materials accelerates, cost of incorporating these materials in new aircraft will drop, and more new aircraft will be built with some measure of stealth, or low-observable, capability.

No one method can guarantee a stealth aircraft's ability to evade detection or to reduce its detectability signature. With the proper blending of radar-, infrared-, visual-, and acoustic-signature reduction techniques, however, and the use of active and passive electronic countermeasures (ECMs), a capable and effective stealth aircraft can be fielded.

RADAR CROSS SECTION

In modern warfare, radar is the most reliable method for detecting aircraft. Reducing an aircraft's radar signature, or its vulnerability to being detected by radar, is thus a key element and perhaps the most important in the application of stealth technology.

During the Vietnam War, American aircraft and aircrews suffered heavy losses from radar-directed SAM missiles. As a result, the aircrews were forced to adopt new countermeasure techniques and new tactics. However, these were stop-gap tactics, designed to counter the situations that arose in Vietnam. If the American military were to gain the offensive advantage when fighting against enemies who were heavily protected with radar, new aircraft incorporating technology that would reduce radar signatures would need to be designed and built.

The first and most important step in reducing an aircraft's radar signature is to reduce its radar cross section (RCS). An aircraft with a small RCS reflects less radar energy and thus has a smaller radar signature than an aircraft with a large RCS.

Techniques used to achieve a small RCS:

◇ Redesign the aircraft's external shape. All of the following have a large RCS: Boxy, angular airframes with many parts joined at right angles; large, open, engine air intakes; and airplanes with a number of flat perpendicular surfaces. The more large, flat surfaces facing the radar, the more radar energy gets reflected back to the radar, making an aircraft with a large RCS easy to detect. A stealth aircraft has curved and nearly flat-angle external surfaces that either absorb radar energy or deflect it away from hostile radar receivers, making the stealth aircraft difficult to locate because it doesn't reflect enough radar energy to the hostile radar.

◇ Make stealth aircraft using composite materials. Plastic, Fiberglas, carbon-carbon, boron, and ceramic composite materials are used for external skins on stealth aircraft, and for coverings over metal structural components. Radar-absorbent materials or paints (RAMs) containing plastic (nonmagnetic), ferrite (magnetically polarized), or retinyl Schiff base salt materials are applied to an airframe to reduce an aircraft's RCS. (More details on how these materials work are given in Chapter 5.)

◇ Increase ECM effectiveness. The smaller an aircraft's RCS, the more effective its ECM equipment because an aircraft with a small RCS reflects only the small amount of radar energy it encounters. Thus, jamming or spoofing (fooling) the hostile radar becomes easier because only the small amount of radar energy that actually reflects back to the hostile radar needs to be altered by ECM equipment.

RCS AND RADAR

An aircraft's RCS represents its ability to be seen or detected by a particular radar and determines the range from the radar from which an aircraft can be detected. An aircraft with an RCS larger than the wavelength of the radar waves being emitted by a radar can be detected by that radar. A successful stealth aircraft will have an RCS smaller than the radar wavelengths it encounters, and thus will be for all practical purposes invisible to that radar (FIG. 3-1 and TABLE 3-1). RCS does vary, however, depending on the angle at which radar energy strikes the aircraft and on the wavelength of the radar, so it is not necessarily a fixed figure for a certain aircraft.

To determine an aircraft's RCS, the amount of radar energy the aircraft reflects back to the radar's receiver is used to determine the size of a reflective sphere that would reflect the same amount of energy. The sphere's size is the aircraft's RCS value.

As just mentioned, the aircraft's RCS also varies with the angle that the radar waves strike the aircraft. Head-on RCS, for instance, would be smaller than the aircraft's RCS if radar waves were directed at the side or bottom of the aircraft. A 1-meter-square flat-plate might have an RCS of 0.01 square meter if it were angled

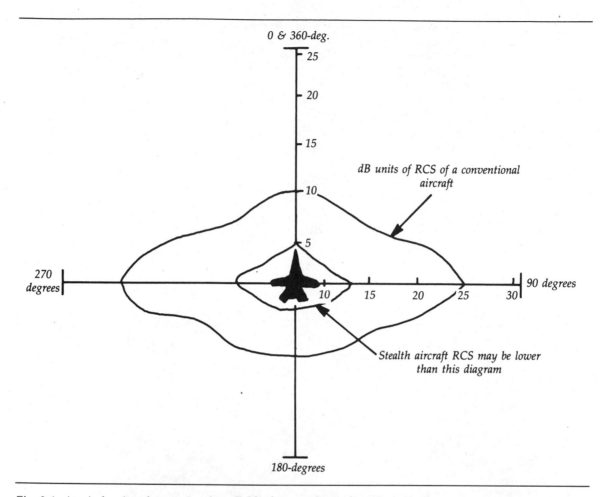

0 & 360-deg.

dB units of RCS of a conventional aircraft

270 degrees

90 degrees

Stealth aircraft RCS may be lower than this diagram

180-degrees

Fig. 3-1. An airplane's radar cross sections (RCS) shows up larger from the sides than the front on a detecting radar screen. Stealth designs have extremely low RCS dB values compared to this diagram.

horizontally to incoming radar energy, but if it were angled vertically to radar energy, the plate would have 1.0 square meter RCS.

Naturally, this feature presents a problem to stealth designers and is the primary reason why radar-absorbent coatings or materials are used on stealth aircraft. It is possible to minimize the flat areas on an aircraft that might be exposed to radar energy, but they can't be eliminated, and their ease of detection by radar must somehow be reduced.

Older generation aircraft, like the B-52 bomber, have huge RCS values, as much as 1,000 square meters (FIG. 3-2). Obviously, then, the B-52 is an unlikely candidate for stealth technology. Other aircraft have varying RCS values. Some stealth aircraft have RCSs beginning at 0.5 square meter, which to a hostile radar could make the aircraft appear smaller than a hummingbird. (FIGURE 3-1 shows an illustration of RCS versus radar wavelength and a listing of typical aircraft RCS values.)

Table 3-1. Radar Cross Sections, in Square Meters, of Selected Aircraft and Missiles.

Type of Aircraft	Radar Cross Section
Bombers	
B-52	1,000 square meters
B-1A	100
B-1B	10
B-2 ATB	0.000001
Fighters	
F-4 Phantom II	100
F-15 Eagle	25
Y-22/23 ATF	0.5
F-117A	0.01
Cruise Missiles	
ALCM	0.25
ACM	0.001

Fig. 3-2. The radar cross section for a B-52 bomber is estimated to be more than 1,000 square meters—extremely large by any standard—and it makes an excellent target for radars. (Courtesy U.S. Air Force)

External shape and RAM coatings are only two important considerations in making an aircraft difficult to detect by radar. Internal structures such as metal spars, ribs, and bulkheads also can reflect radar energy. These parts are constructed so that aspect angles of parts tend to disperse, rather than reflect, radar energy. The parts are coated with RAM to absorb and scatter radar energy. Both of these techniques are used in certain areas on Rockwell's B-1B bomber and throughout the internal structure of Northrop's highly secret Advanced Technology Bomber (ATB).

STEALTH RADARS

Typical aircraft radar antennas are effective radar reflectors themselves. They normally reflect radar energy in the frequency band in which the antenna was designed operate, and this could increase stealth aircraft's chances of being detected by hostile radars.

One type of antenna that has a high RCS signature is the *slotted planar array*, the type most fitted to modern fighter aircraft. However, *conformal phased-array* antennas, which are fitted to the B-1B and B-2 bombers, are considered stealth radars.

The radomes that enclose conformal phased-array radar antenna act as radio-frequency filters. Electromagnetic elements within the walls of the radome itself (sort of "smart-skins") hide the antenna from certain radar frequencies. These special radome radio-frequency filters allow the internal radar to transmit and receive on one frequency while reflecting away other, unwanted, frequencies by employing frequency selective elements within the radome radio-frequency filter system. Some stealth radars are also capable of absorbing radar frequencies other than their own (no reflection).

VISUAL SIGNATURE REDUCTION

Visual detection of aircraft during combat or reconnaissance is usually easy at close range. Part of the effort in stealth technology is to reduce the visual signature of stealth aircraft so stealth missions aren't jeopardized as the aircraft get close to its goals.

Camouflage, or optical decoy, is the most widely used method of reducing an airborne vehicle's visual signature. With the correct application of camouflage colors appropriate to the terrain in which the aircraft will be operating, the aircraft will be better able to blend into the background.

Following are examples of camouflage color schemes used by aircraft designed for specific missions:

Air Superiority. Color and pattern vary. Some types use more than one shade of color and different colors. Colors that might be used on the same aircraft include, for example, light aircraft gray on bottom surfaces, flint gray on upper; dark compass ghost-gray and light compass ghost-gray (found on the F-15, FIG. 3-3); air-superiority blue and light gray.

Bomber, Attack, and Other Aircraft. A color scheme called "European One" has been used on some American military aircraft such as the B1-B and F-15E. Stealth aircraft usually use black or dark ghost-gray color schemes. National insignia found on U.S. stealth or strike aircraft are of the low-visibility type, usually black, red, or gray. They are also small enough so they can't easily be seen.

Other Visual-Signature Reduction Considerations

Reduction of stealth aircraft visual signatures comes naturally with the low-profile RCS-reducing airframe design. If an observer could see it, an effective stealth aircraft with a low-profile cockpit canopy and blended fuselage-wing-engine air intakes would

Fig. 3-3. Two F15s returning from a training mission near Nellis AFB, Nevada. Both are painted in the air-superiority blue gray to blend with their background. (Photo by Ken Hackman, courtesy of U.S. Air Force)

look like a smooth shape with curving lines joining into a continuous form that looks completely unlike a threatening airplane.

As mentioned in Chapter 1, optically transparent materials were tried in the early 1900s in Germany and in the 1930s in Russia without much success. One material that has had some success is a paint that reduces an aircraft's infrared and visual signatures. It was developed by the U.S. Army. In addition to reflecting infrared radiation to lower the infrared signature, the roughly textured paint, combined with special pigments, diffuses sunlight, which aids in blending the aircraft into the background.

Camouflage schemes also have been developed for night and bad-weather operations, specifically to make an aircraft difficult to spot and track using low-light detection devices such as starlight scopes, night-vision goggles, or forward-looking infrared systems (FLIRs). Special coatings have been developed that will not reflect laser light back to laser rangefinders or target seekers.

Little information is available on these camouflage techniques for nocturnal use; the subject is highly classified. It is known, however, that there are lasers and other long-range optical imaging systems that can track stealth aircraft, but in order for these systems to track their target, the target must first be spotted.

Future efforts at visual-signature reduction might include new camouflage techniques that could allow pilots to alter color patterns in flight to match the surrounding terrain, like a chameleon.

Manned stealth aircraft bring up yet another problem: *glint*, or light reflecting off aircraft canopies. Glint generally refers to light reflecting off the entire aircraft, but that can be reduced with special paints. Glint from the cockpit canopy, which pilots would be hard pressed to do without, must be minimized. With the right combination of tint plus some type of polarized laminate, canopy surface-light reflection can be reduced considerably. It also has the benefit of improving pilot vision from the cockpit, especially in hazy conditions. The latest versions of F-15 and F-16 fighters have polarized laminates applied to their canopies.

Contrails and smoke from engines represent another visual signature and could mark the path of a stealth aircraft. Today's engine technology has, for the most part, eliminated the smoke problem by burning fuel more efficiently, but contrails are not so easy to get rid of.

There are three types of contrails:

Aerodynamic: This type of contrail is caused by the reduced pressure of air as it flows past the aircraft. As pressure is reduced, temperature drops, and if the air contains enough moisture and its temperature drops below the dew point of the ambient air, contrails will form.

Convection: Engine exhaust air rises and cools below the dew point of surrounding air, forming a vapor trail.

Engine Exhaust: Moisture-laden engine exhaust expelled into cold air condenses immediately. This type of contrail occurs usually above 30,000 ft. The Air Force said it has solved the contrail problem, but details have not been revealed.

ENGINE INSTALLATION AND INFRARED AND ACOUSTIC SIGNATURE REDUCTION

Engine installation is a crucial factor in reducing detectability signature. Most engines require large amounts of air to operate and are usually placed so that air can flow easily through the engine. The air intake and the face of the exposed jet engine compressor, essentially a large multibladed metal fan, present easily detectable surfaces for hostile radars. Hot engine exhausts normally have large infrared signatures, and engine noise provides yet another means of detection.

These factors can be mitigated by burying the engines inside the fuselage or wing. Conformal or semi-conformal air intakes (FIG. 3-4) allow the engines ready access to air, but are blended into the shape of the fuselage or wing so that radar energy can't reflect off the air intake or the engine's compressor face.

Snake-type ducting is also used in air intakes. Curves in the ducting itself or aerodynamic baffles within the ducting direct airflow smoothly into the engine and at the same time prevent radar energy from entering (FIGS. 3-4 and 3-5).

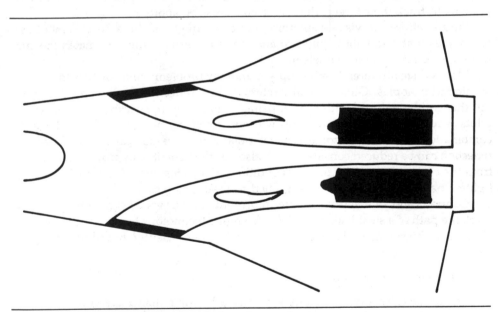

Fig. 3-4. Conformal engine air intake with snake-type ducting.

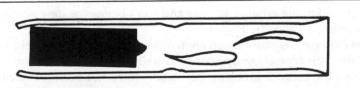

Fig. 3-5. Snake-type engine air intake ducting with internal aerodynamic baffles.

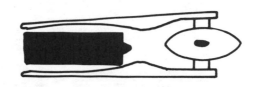

Fig. 3-6. Straight engine air intake with radar-absorbent pitot diffuser (the bulbous fairing on the front of the cowling). Some stealth aircraft engine air intake mouths are covered with a radar screen mesh that prevents radar energy of certain wavelengths from entering the intake ducting.

For older aircraft in which it might be difficult to bury engines inside the airframe, a simple pitot intake can be used. The engine is mounted in a normal fashion, but a radar-absorbent airflow diffuser on the front of the engine keeps radar energy from bouncing off metal engine parts (FIG. 3-6).

To further prevent radar energy from entering engine intakes, stealth designers cover the engine intake with a mesh screen. The mesh is designed to prevent certain radar wavelengths from passing through the mesh into the intake ducting and reflecting back to the radar receiver. One way to do so is for the grids of the mesh to be smaller than the wavelength of incoming radar energy, thus the radar energy can't penetrate the mesh. This is why a glass door can safely be used on a microwave oven. The grids on the oven door screen are smaller than the wavelength of the radar energy being emitted by the oven, thus preventing the energy from escaping and harming a cook standing next to the oven.

The following techniques are primarily aimed at reducing the effects engines have on a stealth aircraft's detectability signature.

Infrared-Signature Reduction

Engines are a primary source of infrared emissions, and for a stealth aircraft to be successful, these emissions must be eliminated or masked. Methods for achieving this goal include shielding, active or passive cooling, and special materials and coatings to absorb or reflect and dissipate infrared radiation. Additional equipment, such as infrared decoy flares, infrared jammers, and other such infrared-signature reducing equipment, also should be incorporated into stealth aircraft design to further reduce the possibility of detection.

The cool air from the fan section of a turbofan engine (FIG. 3-7) can be mixed with hot exhaust gases to reduce infrared emissions. Airflow from the turbine section can be mixed with the inlet airflow, thus increasing inlet air temperature and at the same time reducing exhaust temperature.

Exhaust diffusers, like baffles, can be fitted to the exhaust nozzle (FIG. 3-7B) to further reduce infrared emissions. The baffles separate exhaust flow, allowing the exhaust gases to cool faster. Baffles can be fitted so close together, as on the AH-64 Apache helicopter, that if an infrared-guided missile were able to detect and track the helicopter from its hot exhaust parts, the missile would be blocked by the baffles

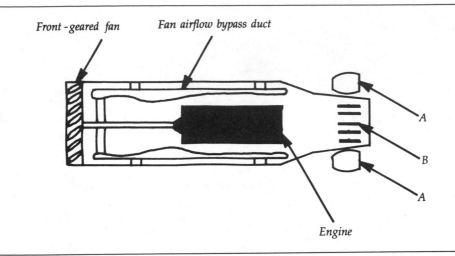

Front-geared fan *Fan airflow bypass duct*

A

B

A

Engine

Fig. 3-7. *Infrared jammers (A) help reduce an engine's infrared signature by emitting flickering infrared signals that confuse infrared guided-missiles and cause them to miss their targets. Engine exhaust cooling baffles (B) help cool engine exhaust gases to keep engine exhaust parts cool enough that they don't attract infrared-guided missiles.*

Fig. 3-8. *A Bell Textron AH-1S Cobra attack helicopter fitted with an exhaust nozzle that directs engine exhaust upward and away from the direct view of most infrared detectors.* (Courtesy of Bell Helicopter TEXTRON)

and would not be able to enter the engine. On some helicopters, the baffles also serve to redirect exhaust gas flow so that infrared emissions are masked and hidden from the ''view'' of hostile weapons (FIGS. 3-8 through 3-10).

The exhaust nozzle itself is designed to minimize infrared emissions by lowering exhaust gas temperatures. Louvers and bypass valves mix direct-inlet airflow with cool ambient air and exhaust gases to continue the exhaust cooling process. An active cooling system is another method and might consist of an aft fan stage within the exhaust nozzle.

Infrared jammers are mounted near exhaust nozzles (FIG. 3-7A) to confuse hostile infrared detection and missile-guidance systems. These jammers are used on the B1-B bomber and consist of a device that emits strong flickering infrared radiation, which confuses an infrared-guided missile into thinking it is off track. The missile corrects its course based on the new information it is receiving, and so misses its target.

Infrared detection and guidance systems actually home in on the outside of the hot exhaust nozzle, not the exhaust plume itself. In most stealth designs, either exhaust nozzles are shielded by the airframe's angled vertical fins or the engines are installed so that the nozzles are forward of the wing trailing edge. Both options make it more

Fig. 3-9. An infrared-signature suppressor and infrared jammer, fitted to an AH-1S Huey Cobra attack helicopter. The suppressor, developed by Bell, consists of exhaust baffles that mix the exhaust gases with air, thus cooling the exhaust and reducing IR emissions. Seen above and slightly forward of the IR suppressor baffle is an IR jammer also developed by Bell Helicopters. The jammer sends out flickering infrared signals that confuse infrared-tracking missiles and cause them to miss their target. (Courtesy of Bell Helicopter)

Fig. 3-10. The UH-60 Quick Fix electronic intelligence and radio communication jamming helicopter. Note the nonstandard infrared-signature reducing engine exhaust and cooling nozzles. (Courtesy U.S. Army)

difficult for infrared detection and guidance systems to engage a stealth aircraft.

Inside the engine bay, mirror-finish gold and silver films reflect internal infrared radiation produced by the engine. High-density carbon-carbon foams or grains can be packed around the engines and into cavities to absorb infrared radiation from the engine and also radar energy entering the air intake. Ceramic materials coating the outside of the engine bay dissipate infrared radiation and, as a side benefit, preserve the surfaces, usually titanium, to which they are applied.

A RAM coating called *iron ball* also comes in handy inside the engine bay because it not only absorbs radar energy, but it also absorbs infrared radiation and distributes it evenly over the surface to which it is applied, after which the infrared radiation dissipates. (More information about iron ball follows in Chapter 5.)

Just as the development of radar advanced quickly during World War II, so too did the development of early infrared detection and guidance systems in the same time period. Today, infrared detection, tracking, and guidance systems have progressed to an advanced stage of effectiveness. Some infrared detection sensors used in fighter aircraft can spot the infrared radiation from a cigarette 50 miles away. In the future, there most probably will be satellites that will be able to detect and track aircraft from their infrared emissions. Some of the more advanced infrared-guided antiaircraft missiles use imaging infrared guidance and other imaging techniques that probably can engage some stealth aircraft, even those with reduced infrared signatures. Infrared detection systems can be fooled, occasionally, by infrared decoy flares and also by certain environmental conditions.

Infrared radiation is shorter in wavelength, but higher in frequency, than radar energy (microwave radiation). Infrared wavelengths lie between 0.72 and 1,000 microns on the electromagnetic spectrum, or between 300,000 and 400 million megahertz. In discussions on the absorption and emission of infrared radiation, the term *black body* is used to define an object that will absorb any and all radiation falling upon it, with no reflection.

The term *emissivity* is defined as the ratio of total radiation emitted by an object at a certain temperature to total radiation that would be emitted by a perfect black body at the same temperature. An object's emissivity depends on the amount of energy its surface can absorb. If a particular surface will absorb most of the energy striking it, engine heat for example, then the surface's emissivity is high, and the surface in this case will get hot and be easily detectable by infrared-guided missiles. If the same surface reflects most or all of the infrared radiation striking it, then the surface will emit small amounts of infrared radiation and will have a low emissivity and a low infrared signature.

Emissivity is markedly different for various materials (TABLE 3-2), a silvered mirror having the lowest emission level. A black body at 27.2 degrees centigrade will radiate 46 milliwatts of power per square centimeter of its surface. The painted surface of an aircraft at the same temperature will radiate 41 milliwatts per square centimeter. If the aircraft were not painted and had a bare aluminum skin, it would emit less than 4 milliwatts per square centimeter.

Infrared radiation produced by a turbine exhaust or rocket engine exhaust plume, while not as crucial as the infrared signature from hot engine parts, is a factor that must be minimized. This type of infrared radiation is caused by molecular excitation of water vapor and carbon dioxide, both of which are by-products of combustion. This radiation peaks at about 2.7 microns for water vapor mixed with carbon dioxide and 4.3 microns for the carbon dioxide alone. It is considered important for stealth

	Surface	Emissivity
Table 3-2. Emissivity of Selected Surfaces.	Black body	1.00
	Lampblack	0.95
	Painted (or coated)	0.90
	Cold rolled steel	0.60
	Aluminum paint	0.25
	Stainless steel	0.09
	Aluminum aircraft skin	0.08
	Aluminum foil	0.04
	Silvered mirror	0.02

designers to reduce emissivity of stealth aircraft engine infrared radiation to below 2.0 microns in order to reduce the chance of infrared-guided missiles hitting the aircraft.

It is interesting to note that, although a visually reflective surface is not desirable from visual- and radar-signature reduction standpoints, it is desirable for reduced infrared signature reduction. This is just one of the many compromises stealth designers must deal with in their quest for ''invisible'' aircraft.

Acoustic-Signature Reduction

Aircraft engines are noisy, and so are propeller blades and helicopter rotor blades. If a stealth aircraft can't be detected by radar or infrared tracking systems or by sighting, at some point it will probably be audible to hostile forces.

Noise is most pronounced in turbine engines. Several commercial and military programs have been underway for many years to reduce the noise produced by turbine engines.

FIGURE 3-11 shows a conversion developed by Page Avjet Corp., of Orlando, Florida, for the Pratt & Whitney JT3D-3B engine. This engine was used for many early commercial airliners, including Boeing's venerable 707. The conversion, called the Quiet Nacelle Noise Reduction modification, cuts noise emitted by the engine in two ways: by absorbing high-frequency harmonic vibrations produced by the high-speed airflow exhausted from the primary fan nozzles, and by dampening noise generated by the rotating stages of the engine. An acoustically treated engine inlet, center body, and bifurcated duct are installed, but no modification to the main engine cowling is required.

The air intake cowl is modified with an acoustically treated inner facing, and the center body is remanufactured using sound-absorbing materials. Both remain the same size as the orginial. The original bifurcated duct is modified with a liner consisting

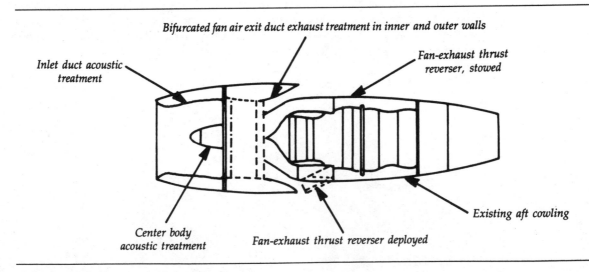

Fig. 3-11. Reducing the aural signature.

of Nomex honeycomb and preimpregnated graphite fabric. Nomex honeycomb sandwiched between layers of graphite fabric, Fiberglas, and perforated aluminum is used in various places. The pattern of perforations, hole size, and material-layering sequence vary, depending on the harmonic frequency to be absorbed and the structural requirements of each component.

Stealth acoustic-signature reduction technology is more advanced, but also uses some of the techniques described for infrared-signature reduction. Several new methods have been developed to further reduce the acoustic signatures of military aircraft engines. They include the use of screech liners in afterburners and sandwich composite skins with pyramidal structures pointing inward to absorb engine noise. Use of baffles and louvers in areas where airflow is noisy also helps to reduce engine noise.

Procedures that reduce acoustic signatures also contribute to minimizing infrared signatures. Laminated coatings on the exhaust nozzle, for instance, reduce infrared and acoustic signatures.

For piston engines, modified mufflers are used to reduce engine noise. Lockheed's YO-3A quiet reconnaissance aircraft used during the Vietnam War had an extremely quiet exhaust system, as well as a slow-turning propeller that emitted very little noise.

RADIO-FREQUENCY EMISSION AND LEAKAGE

After the major culprits that make aircraft easy to detect are taken care of, another important problem shows up: radio-frequency emission and leakage from on-board avionics systems that could make a stealth aircraft an easy target. Emissions and leakage can be reduced or eliminated by shielding the leaky equipment with RAM placed around avionics bays. Boron-type composites and ferrite-based coatings (Chapter 5) are best for preventing internal radio-frequency leakage and are also used to harden or shield avionics from destructive electromagnetic pulses resulting from nuclear explosions.

If a stealth aircraft is equipped with radar, the radar should be operated in nonstandard modes so that its emissions won't be detected. One method is to operate the radar with intermediate pulsing, as well as incorporate techniques to eliminate side-lobe leakage and beam scatter. The radar antenna must be shielded from incoming radar energy, yet also be able to transmit and receive radar energy; this might be difficult and require unorthodox design techniques.

Chapter Four

Advanced Stealth Design Considerations and Operational Techniques

RADAR ENERGY DOES NOT REFLECT SMOOTHLY FROM A TARGET, BUT usually scatters after hitting a target. The more-pronounced scattered waves, some of which bounce back to the radar receiver, are what enable radar to detect the target. The less-pronounced waves are called *side lobes* and can also sometimes be detected as well. Stealth technology's main function is to reduce, eliminate, or scatter even further any reflected radar energy so that radar receivers won't be able to detect what little reflected energy remains.

A research team at Sperry Corp. conducted a study to attempt to develop smooth radar reflections from scattered radar energy reflected by various aircraft models. These models featured a variety of aerodynamic configurations and had cylindrical fuselages with triangular- or quadrilateral-shaped wings and stabilizers. Scattered radar reflection response was tested for the models before and after they were coated with RAM.

It was found that RAM reduced scatter response (reflected energy), but that the amount of reduction depended on the spectrum of radar energy and the model's *aspect angle*, or the angle at which the radar energy was directed at the model. The results of the tests showed that RAM reduces RCS by *attenuating*, or lessening, the magnitude of the target's reflectivity.

One area of the plane where reflectivity is often strong is in engine bay cavities, which tend to become resonant chambers when illuminated by radar. Dipoles installed in an engine bay cavity interact with the radar energy and disperse the energy. When properly positioned in the cavity, the dipoles *defocus*, or scatter, the energy at various angles, thus reducing the RCS of the cavity. Carbon-carbon porous foam (see Chapter 5) is a form of RAM used in engine bay cavities and is just as effective as dipoles in attenuating or dissipating radar energy.

Sharp external airframe angles are also good reflectors of radar energy, but CAD techniques make it possible to reduce RCS by designing an airframe that tends to scatter and disperse radar energy instead of reflecting it back to the radar receiver (FIGS.4-1 through 4-3). Recent stealth designs from Lockheed include small flat surfaces with high aspect angles to the radar illumination; these surfaces are excellent side-lobe attenuators.

The radar reflection of Lockheed's F-117A stealth fighter is said to look fuzzy, like porcupine quills, on radar screens, but only when the aircraft is close enough to the radar to be detected—reportedly, at 20 miles or less.

Aircraft that haven't been designed for the stealth mission from the start can still benefit from stealth technology. RCS of a nonstealth aircraft can be greatly reduced using RAM coatings, and nonstealth aircraft that have been treated with RAM include the F-15 and F-16 fighters and the B-1B bomber (FIGS. 4-4 AND 4-5)

One of the earliest aircraft to employ a combination of stealth techniques is Lockheed's SR-71 Blackbird reconnaissance airplane. The SR-71 can be seen visually long before it can be detected by radar, due to its low RCS from special external shaping and efficient use of RAM and ECM equipment. (FIGURE 4-6 illustrates radar-defeating construction incorporated into the SR-71's wing leading edges and fuselage skin strakes.)

The effectiveness of the SR-71's stealth equipment was demonstrated in a series of tests, in which an F-14 Tomcat and F-15 Eagle flew mock intercepts on an SR-71 flying at high altitude. The tracking radars in the F-14 and F-15 were not able to lock on to the SR-71. Both fighters' radars were set in the look-up/shoot-down mode (FIGS. 4-7 and 4-8).

While the goal of stealth technology is to make aircraft "invisible," in certain cases a stealth aircraft can be readily visible to radar. Older low-frequency early warning radars have wavelengths large enough to resolve stealth-equipped aircraft. Newer

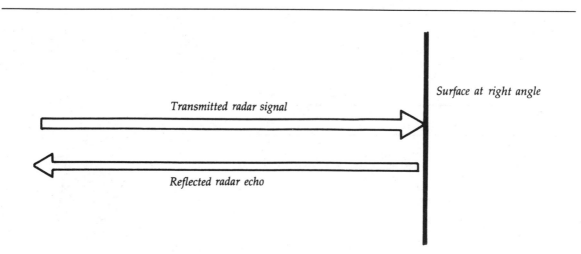

Fig. 4-1. A flat surface at a right angle to incoming radar energy makes an excellent radar reflector and thus is easily detectable. It has a high radar signature.

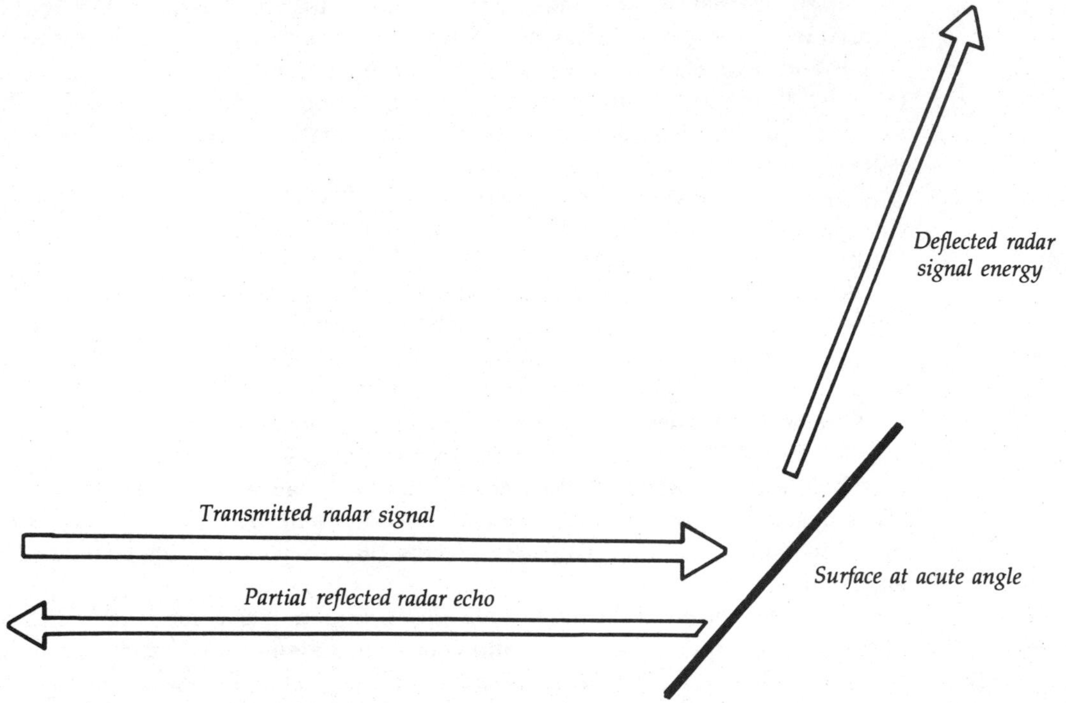

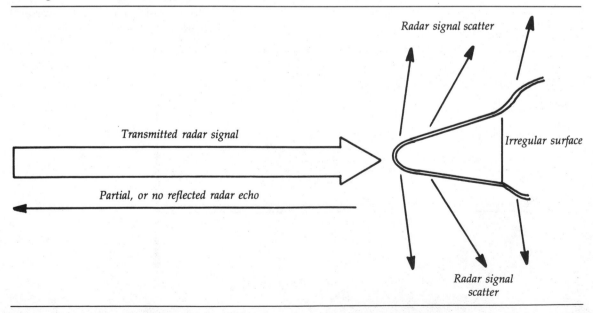

Fig. 4-2. *An angled surface deflects some of the incoming radar energy away from the radar receiver and thus has smaller radar signature, but is still detectable.*

Fig. 4-3. *The lowest radar signature belongs to an irregular surface, in which much of the incoming radar energy is deflected and little reflects back to the radar receiver. This surface has the lowest radar signature.*

Fig. 4-4. General Dynamics F-16B trainer/fighter with undersides painted with a special camouflage coating. The paint is highly infrared reflective and diffuses sunlight, thus helping the aircraft blend more easily into the background. (Courtesy U.S. Air Force)

Fig. 4-5. The Air Force's B-1B bomber. Engine nacelles, the square portions under each wing, are fitted with snake-type baffles that hide the engine's metal compressor faces from incoming radar energy. (Courtesy Rockwell International)

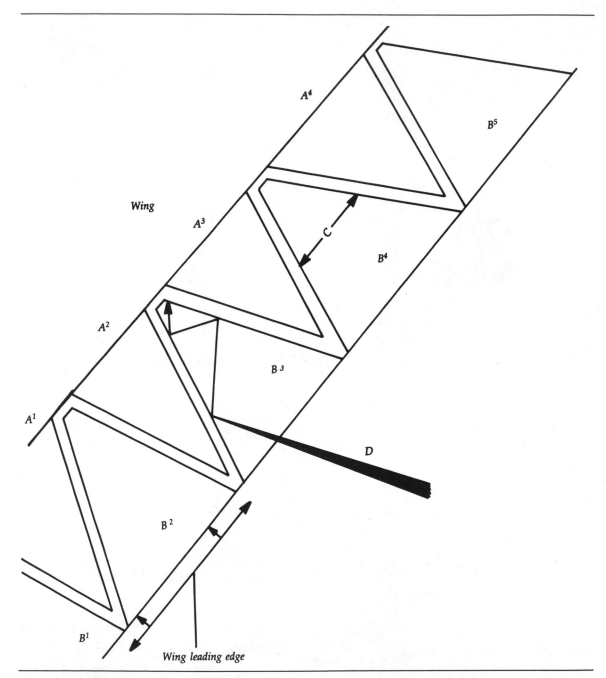

Fig. 4-6. *A typical wing leading edge design that sharply reduces RCS used on Lockheed's SR-71 and Northrop's B-2 advanced technology bomber. Triangular titanium radar reflectors (A1 to A4) are set at an angle to incoming radar energy. Super-plastic RAM developed by Lockheed is fitted into the cavities formed by the titanium triangles (B1 to B5). Radar reflector plates (C) deflect incoming radar energy (D) and keep it trapped in radar-absorbent plastic (B). Incoming radar energy (D) is deflected and trapped in a triangular cavity filled with plastic RAM.*

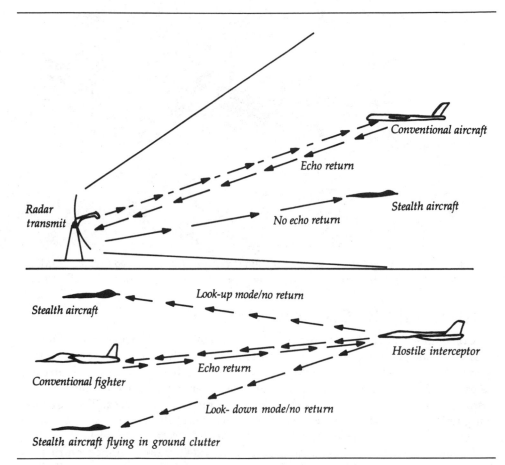

Fig. 4-7. (top) A simple example of how ground-based radar transmitters seek and detect aircraft and how a stealth aircraft can remain undetected. (bottom) An effective stealth aircraft will return no reflected radar energy to a hostile aircraft, thus avoiding detection.

high-frequency radars used in tracking and guidance radars aren't able to engage stealth aircraft as easily because of their smaller radar energy wavelengths, as well as some other factors. Tracking and guidance radars, for instance, can't distinguish between reflected radar signals from stealth aircraft and the signal from background clutter when the radar is being used in look-down mode (FIG. 4-7).

Soviet tracking and guidance radars (usually J-band) lack the sophisticated microprocessor technology needed to process the vast amount of information that is received as reflected radar signals. It is only with microprocessors that the Soviets would be able to resolve a stealth aircraft's reflection against background clutter. Without the necessary computing power, the low-tech radar cope would be blank and would not show any information on the stealth aircraft.

However, on missions against countries that use an older low-frequency radar, a stealth aircraft might need to use other methods to avoid detection, or, as the saying goes, "If you can't be stealthy, then be sneaky."

Fig. 4-8. *Grumman/Navy F-14A Tomcat fighter aircraft carrying six active-radar-guided AIM-54 Phoenix antiaircraft missiles. Note the optic/infrared sensor under the nose of the aircraft.* (Courtesy U.S. Navy)

LOW-LEVEL RADAR AVOIDANCE

Conventional aircraft have used various low-level flying techniques to avoid hostile radar for years, and in some cases stealth aircraft also might employ these techniques. Even though a stealth aircraft might be all but undetectable by hostile radar, an extra margin of safety and invisibility can be realized if the aircraft flies low enough to avoid hostile radar, thus increasing the chances of the missions's success. The low-level flying techniques, usually carried out within 500 feet of the ground, are known as *jinking, snaking,* or *nap-of-the-earth* or *terrain/contour following* (FIG. 4-9).

Passive microwave or laser radar is used to provide terrain-clearance information for the aircraft, allowing it to hug the ground as it streaks toward its target—climbing over hills and mountains and dropping quickly into valleys—to remain clear of hostile radar searches. Aircraft operating at high speeds close to the ground are equipped with autostabilization and automatic ride-control devices to smooth the often violently rough ride at such low altitudes.

Conventional aircraft flying at low levels can avoid hostile early warning radar quite successfully, but must be careful to avoid detection by enemy interceptor aircraft or airborne warning and control system (AWACS) radar-platform aircraft equipped with pulse-Doppler (S-band) radar operated in the look-down/shoot-down mode (FIGS. 4-10 and 4-11).

A stealth aircraft, on the other hand, with an RCS smaller than the wavelength of the interceptor's look-down radar and the ground-based early-warning radar and flying at low levels, could easily avoid detection. The optimum time for low-level stealth operations is at night, preferably after midnight.

The U.S. Navy's Advanced Air-to-Air Missile (AAAM) development will use "new technology" that will enable it to engage stealth-type targets. This technology apparently incorporates a breakthrough in sensor and signal processing systems. The U.S. Air Force also might use the AAAM, since its newest air-to-air missile, the

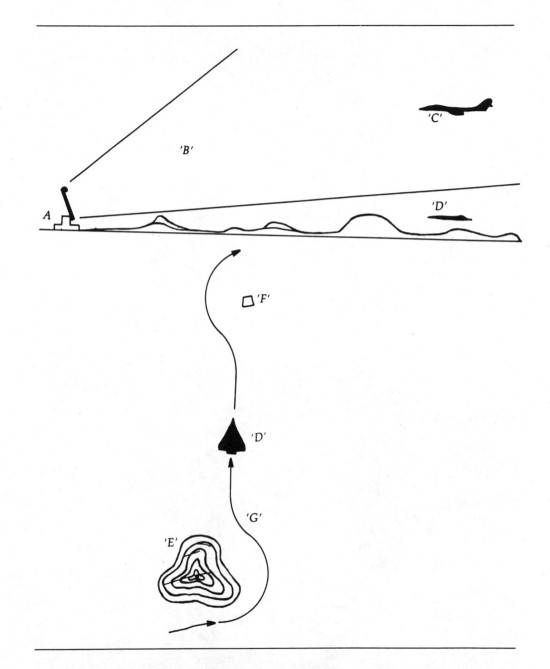

Fig. 4-9 (top) Aircraft C is easily detected by radar transmitter A, while aircraft D avoids radar by flying below radar energy. This is referred to as nap-of-the-earth *flying, terrain following, or jinking, and requires that the aircraft be flown at high speeds close to the ground to avoid detection. Although a stealth aircraft might be able to avoid detection by radar merely by virtue of its low RCS, its chances of completing its mission increase greatly if it also flies nap of the Earth. The bottom illustration shows a terrain-following aircraft and the path it might take around some obstacles. Most such flying is done within 500 feet of the ground.*

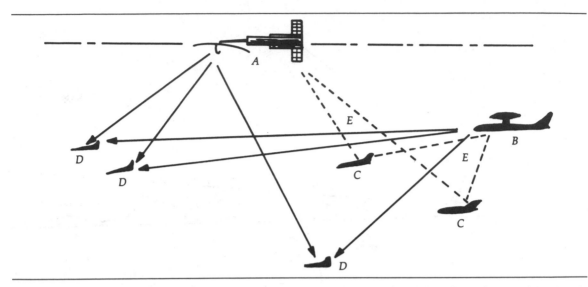

Fig. 4-10. With space-based radar (A) friendly fighters' radar (C) can be used as bistatic receivers to detect hostile intruders (D). Friendly fighters also get information on intruders from AWACS (B) via secure digital datalinks (E).

Fig. 4-11. An E-3A Sentinel airborne warning and control system (AWACS) aircraft over the Philippines. An airborne radar detection system such as that used in the Sentinel can easily detect conventional attacking aircraft, even if they are flying low in an attempt to avoid detection by ground-based radars. Stealth aircraft, however, should be able to sneak by AWACS-type aircraft without being detected. (Courtesy U.S. Air Force)

AIM-120 AMRAAM, does not have the Navy AAAM's stealth-buster technology. The AAAM will have the ability to engage what has been termed emerging Soviet stealth technology.

If the Soviets deploy more advanced systems and newer radar detection and tracking equipment, then American stealth designers will need to develop new techniques to counter increasingly sophisticated Soviet systems. The U.S. military should not wait until Soviets develop effective stealth systems, but should proceed with efforts to find solutions to counter future Soviet stealth vehicles and systems.

STEALTH AND ECM

ECM equipment installed on a low-RCS stealth aircraft can contribute a great deal to making the aircraft harder to detect. The lower the stealth aircraft's RCS, the less power will be needed by the ECM equipment to *jam* (burn through) and *spoof* (fool) the hostile radar. The less radar energy reflected by the aircraft, the less power will be needed to alter the energy to fool the hostile radar.

Today's sophisticated ECM equipment can intercept hostile radar energy, analyze it, cross-match it with on-board information, and retransmit a similar, but delayed signal that will give the hostile radar operator false position information. By the time the radar operator notes the information on his scope, the stealth aircraft will be many miles away from where the operator believes the aircraft to be.

STEALTH-BUSTERS

There are radar systems on the drawing board or in testing that might prove capable of detecting, tracking, and guiding weapons against stealth aircraft (FIGS. 4-12 and 4-13).

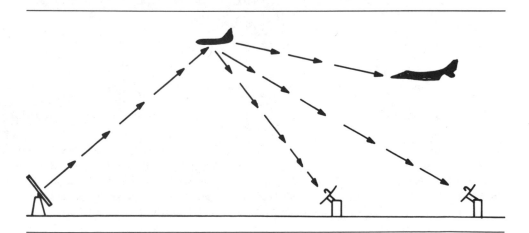

Fig. 4-12 Bistatic radar—where the radar receiver is located away from the transmitter, in this case in an aircraft—might eventually become an effective means of detecting stealth aircraft.

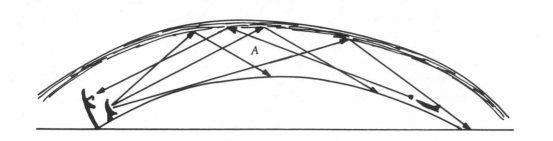

Fig. 4-13. *Over-the-horizon backscatter radar can detect targets over the horizon by bouncing radar energy off the ionosphere.*

Fig. 4-14. *If a stealth aircraft is having trouble avoiding detection, the EF-111A Raven radar-jamming aircraft can be helpful. This Raven is shown positioned for refueling by an aerial tanker and is based at RAF Upper Heyford in Great Britain. The Raven can defeat any known Soviet radar used to direct surface-to-air missiles (SAMs) and antiaircraft gunfire, and it is also effective against Soviet guidance radars. (Courtesy U.S. Air Force)*

Fig. 4-15. The McDonnell Douglas F-4G Wild Weasel air-defense suppression aircraft. Used in conjunction with the EF-111A Raven, the F-4G provides friendly aircraft an almost weapons-free path to and from intended targets by attacking SAM sites with a variety of air-to-surface weapons. These weapons include the AGM-65 Maverick, 500-pound iron bombs (including precision-guided types), Shrike missiles, and antiradiation missiles such as the AGM-78, AGM-88, and Northrop AGM-136A Tacit Rainbow. Operating in conjunction with the F-4G and the EF-111A, a stealth aircraft could attack targets without suffering any damage. This F-4G is based at George AFB in California. (Courtesy U.S. Air Force)

Previously, there was some circumstantial evidence that the Soviets were developing their own stealth program, U.S. defense intelligence officials having stated that "the Soviets might have already developed aircraft with a low radar cross section." This was confirmed during July 1988, when the Soviets invited several American military personnel to visually inspect a Soviet stealth aircraft in the USSR. One of the U.S. officials was allowed to look inside the cockpit area of the Soviet stealth plane.

Although Soviet stealth developments do not seem to be as advanced as American stealth programs, the Defense Advanced Research Projects Agency (DARPA) and the Air Force are developing stealth countermeasures in case the emerging Soviet stealth program is successful.

Radars capable of searching through the full radio-frequency spectrum can overcome some types of RAM by using a frequency that isn't addressed by the RAM.

Most Soviet airborne and early-warning radars (in interceptors and AWACS-type aircraft) operate in J-band frequencies. Their anti-aircraft missiles (AAMs) employ monopulse semiactive radar guidance, and some newer missiles use active radar guidance in the pulse-Doppler mode. Their surface-to-air missiles (SAMs) operate in J-band frequencies. These represent the threats that the U.S. stealth program is designed to counter (FIGS. 4-14 and 4-15).

Millimeter-Wave Radiometry

One possible stealth countermeasure—a system that could be used to detect stealth aircraft—is *millimeter-wave radiometry*, or the measurement of radiation in the infrared, visible, and ultraviolet regions of the electromagnetic spectrum. This kind of system has sensors that can detect objects reflected against a background with a higher or lower temperature than the object. A stealth aircraft might show warm against a cold sky as viewed from below, for instance, or cold against the warm earth as viewed from above.

Imaging Infrared Sensors

An imaging infrared sensor with large focal-plane arrays could be used to track aircraft with low infrared signatures.

Thermal Imaging Sensor

Closely akin to an infrared optical sensor is a new type called a *thermal imaging sensor* (TIS), which can sense both hot and cool areas of any given target, whether it be of conventional or stealth design. Unlike an infrared sensor, however, the TIS can "see" through mist, smoke, darkness, haze, light fog, and rain, and is not affected by low-level background IR radiation, which has hampered most IR sensors seeking targets, especially in the look-down mode. The TIS can also "see" through camouflage.

The thermal imaging sensor also can discriminate between target and decoy much better than infrared sensors. DARPA has been evaluating the thermal imaging sensor technology to identify different aircraft targets, and with the aid of artificial intelligence, to see if the thermal imaging sensor can tell a MiG-29 Fulcrum from an F-15 Eagle, for example.

There is a down side to effectively employing thermal imaging sensors to detect ground-based targets. Targets to be hidden from the thermal sensor can employ a number of countermeasures, such as:

◇ Thermal sensors can be "spoofed" by decoys or blinded by false signals.
◇ Thermal imaging sensors can be spoofed by a British-developed antithermal smoke screen. Called Visual and Infrared Screening Smoke (*VIRSS*), it employs a substance to provide infrared "hotspots" within the smoke itself, as well as provide an absorbent quality. VIRSS reportedly can provide protection against thermal sensors operating in the 3- to 5- and 8- to 14-micron range.

◇ Thermal sensors can be blocked by special camouflage netting. This netting screens the item's own infrared radiation and only allows undetectable warm air to be emitted. In conjunction with this camouflaging, the item might employ another thermal net to emit an infrared signature that matches the surrounding infrared background.

Whether or not stealth aircraft makes use of these, or similar, techniques to avoid being detected by thermal imaging sensors is not known.

Radio-Frequency Sensor

A sensor that employs methods developed for radio astronomy could be used as a passive sensor. Such sensors would be based on the principle that an object that gives off infrared radiation produces a corresponding radio signal. It is the same principle that allows astronomers to learn the temperatures of stars and planets. A stealth aircraft flying through the air would not be able to avoid aerodynamic heating of the air it passes through, and thus would emit radio signals that could be picked up by a sensitive passive sensor. In this kind of sensor, signal-to-noise ratio is very important and will need to be at low enough levels for the sensor to detect radio-frequency emission produced by aerodynamic heating of an aircraft in flight. Although these radio frequency emissions are relatively small compared to background noise, this type of sensor might be viable, given enough research and development.

Bistatic Radar

A bistatic radar transmits radar energy that is reflected from a target and received by receivers in locations apart from the transmitter. These are passive receivers that can be located on land, ships, or aircraft, and that can guide weapons against stealth targets without being detected.

Magnetic Anomaly Detector

To track stealth aircraft, a magnetic anomaly detector (MAD) would have to be more sophisticated than the types used to detect submarines. MADs are used to show the position of submarines by detecting distortions in the Earth's magnetic field by the submarines' steel hulls. Aluminum and its alloys distort the Earth's magnetic field much less than does the steel in submarines, but a sensitive enough MAD might be able to reveal the location of a stealth aircraft.

Laser/Gas Spectrometer Sensor

A laser/gas spectrometer sensor would be able to detect and tract exhaust gases from engines of stealth aircraft. It would use technology similar to that developed for gas spectrometers and lasers.

Doppler Radar

Engineers speculate that, since wing vortices generated by aircraft can be detected by high-definition Doppler radar, it might be possible to use a similar radar to detect a stealth aircraft.

Carrier-Free Radar

Not yet fully developed, this type of radar technique is said to defeat certain types of radar-absorbent materials. The technique involves a radar that generates pulses of radar energy simultaneously in frequencies spanning the entire (or almost) radar spectrum. This type of radar is more advanced than the latest pulse Doppler, or frequency agile types, which might employ many different frequencies in operation, but only one frequency at a time. The carrier-free radar, with its omni-frequency capability, has waves that are square to rectangular in form and will not be absorbed by RAMs. The carrier-free radar waves, therefore, will be reflected.

In most stealth aircraft designs, the precision fitting of parts (of RAMs) is very crucial to the aircraft's RCS value. If the parts are not fitted to extremely close tolerances, radar reflective "hot-spots" will result and will increase the RCS value of the stealth aircraft. Computer-aided-design (CAD) and computer-aided manufacturing (CAM) techniques were employed in the design and production of the B-2 and F-117 stealth aircraft. One technique employed by Lockheed for producing the F-117 stealth fighter is called *faceting* and achieves excellent results at eliminating the so-called radar reflective "hot-spots."

In fact, all the techniques mentioned in this and the previous chapter—RCS-reducing shape and RAM coatings; infrared-, acoustic-, and visual-signature reduction; ECM; low-level radar-avoidance flying—factors that must be taken into account in designing a successful, hard-to-detect stealth aircraft. The techniques can be used individually, but the ultimate success of a stealth aircraft—whether or not it can be detected and can complete its mission—depends on a skillful blending of stealth techniques that combine to make a stealth aircraft an effective military weapon.

Chapter Five

Stealth Materials

MANY DIFFERENT MATERIALS ARE USED IN STEALTH DESIGN, WHICH IS one reason stealth technology is so expensive. The materials are key ingredients in the stealth cookbook and must fulfill the demanding task of attenuating, absorbing, dissipating, and scattering the many types of radiation or radar energy encountered by an aircraft or given off by the aircraft itself.

With the recent advances in composite (nonmetallic) materials, stealth technology has become more viable and realistic. Some of the materials used in stealth aircraft include pure composites, composites combined with metal, coated metal, synthetic materials, glass fibers embedded in plastic, ceramic materials, and special paints and RAM coatings. Few aircraft are being built using only composites, so it is likely that any structural or systems-related metal parts that remain in a stealth airframe will need to be coated with RAM to maintain stealth standards.

Stealth technology has been driven by military needs, specifically by the U.S. Air Force and the Defense Advanced Research Projects Agency, and many companies have responded to the challenge. Although materials for stealth aircraft certainly can be used for ordinary commercial or military aircraft, the pressing need for undetectable stealth aircraft has stimulated a great deal of research on materials that are suitable for stealth aircraft. Entities and companies involved in this work include the Air Force's Materials Laboratory, Dow Chemical Co., Du Pont Chemical Co., Lockheed Corp., Ciba-Geigy Corp., Arco Metals Co., and a number of smaller companies and research laboratories.

EARLY DEVELOPMENTS

Near the end of World War II, the U.S. military developed a RAM coating called MX-410. This material was somewhat effective, but primitive and heavy. Too many coats added too much weight to an aircraft, and in some cases, the treated aircraft became too heavy to fly.

The U.S. military was still interested in stealth technology, however, and classified research continued, with some prototype stealth aircraft flying in the early 1970s. Lockheed and Northrop were heavily involved with early stealth programs and gained considerable experience in the field. The two companies' prototypes also gained much press attention between 1977 and 1982. Boeing, Rockwell, General Dynamics, and LTV are also believed to have built stealth prototypes, including both flight and static, or wind tunnel test, articles.

Crucial Composites

Composite materials are now beginning to replace metal throughout aircraft structures, leading to lighter and stronger airframes. A side benefit of composite materials is that they contribute greatly to reducing an aircraft's RCS and its infrared and acoustic signatures. Materials for stealth aircraft are chosen for their ability to absorb and dissipate microwave (radar) or infrared radiation. Composites of carbon, boron, silicon, and materials such as ceramics and super-plastics are excellent radar energy absorbers.

One material, called the *Jaumann absorber*, consists of laminated layers of a composite material separated by a dielectric spacer material. Jaumann absorber is reportedly difficult to manufacture, but it has been developed to the point where it can be used with a reasonable degree of accuracy and effectiveness.

In order for a material to absorb radar energy, it usually consists of a composite layer that is transparent to the radar energy. Under the composite layer, a metal layer—possibly a metal/composite matrix—attenuates or scatters the radar energy so that the energy doesn't reflect back from the aircraft, but dissipates so as not to reveal the aircraft's position. Note that any substance or material that absorbs energy will show an increase in temperature as a result of the energy absorption.

Aluminum Oxide Fibers. Used in metal-matrix or hybrid composites with an aramid fiber mixture.

Aramid Fibers. Aromatic polyamide fibers used in resin-matrix composites.

Boron. Large-diameter boron fibers for use in matrix resin and metal matrix composites can be made by vapor deposition of boron on tungsten filaments. Boron fibers can be coated with boron carbide for use in metal matrix composites.

Carbon-carbon Composite. Used in areas of high temperature; has both good infrared radiation dissipation and radar energy absorption qualities. Dense carbon grain and ultradense carbon foam (pure pitch) are used in engine areas to absorb heat from the engine exhaust. Carbon-carbon composites can be formed into wing leading-edge panels, and nose and tail cones. Carbon-reinforced Fiberglas material, developed by the Air Force, is used in some air-launched cruise missiles.

Carbon Fibers. Made from pitch for use in resin-matrix composites.

Ceramics. Excellent radar-energy transparent material, making it an ideal dielectric substance. Also acts effectively as an infrared radiation dissipater when applied as a coating.

Fibaloy. Developed by Dow Chemical Co.; produced by embedding glass fibers in plastic. This material reportedly is strong enough for use as external aircraft skin and for some internal structural members, without metal reinforcement. Fibaloy, which is black, is thought to be the chief material being used on Lockheed's stealth strike/reconnaissance airplane and is also reportedly used on the many remotely piloted vehicles (RPVs) that Lockheed manufactures. Fibaloy has excellent radar-energy absorbency qualities.

Fiberglas Epoxy Resin Composites. Simplest radar-energy transparent material; used in some stealth aircraft and in many commerical aircraft.

Kevlar 49. A Du Pont product; possible replacement for carbon-fiber composites in structural applications. Kevlar 49 is an aramid fiber-based composite that is stronger and lighter than some metals and an excellent radar energy absorber. A commercial version of Kevlar also absorbs radar energy and is damage-resistant to gunfire. Du Pont produes other composites that may be used in stealth aircraft, including Fiber FP/Aluminum and Fiber FP/Magnesium.

Metals. Metals that will most likely be used in stealth airframes include a lightweight lithium-aluminum alloy, high-temperature aluminum-metal matrix composites, and to replace expensive titanium in areas where temperatures rise above 290 degrees centigrade, a powder metallurgy aluminum-iron-cerium alloy.

Silag. A metal-composite produced by Arco Metals Co. Rice hulls are baked at high temperatures until they break down into carbon and silicon-carbide whiskers. These whiskers are mixed with aluminum powder to form Silag composite. Silag can be used for an aircraft's structural members. Radar-absorbent capabilities of Silag are minimal, but the material is effective for some specific radar wavelengths.

Silicon-Carbide Fibers. A silicon material, effective at reducing the infrared signature of a stealth aircraft's engines. Similar to tiles used on belly and wing leading edges of U.S. space shuttles for heat dissipation during atmospheric reentry from Earth orbit. Silicon-carbide fibers are also used in metal-matrix composites.

Spectra-100. Developed by Allied Corp., this material is 50 percent stronger than Kevlar, and has high strength-to-weight ratio. Similar radar-energy absorption features as Kevlar.

Super-plastics. Developed by the Air Force Materials Laboratory and commercial firms, super-plastics are thermoplastics that are lighter and stronger than steel and titanium, but do not reflect radar energy. One application of thermoplastics is thought to be a black fiber-reinforced graphite skin used for the wing leading edges of Northrop's B-2A Advanced Technology Bomber.

One class of thermoplastics is known as *ordered polymers* and was developed by the Air Force Materials Laboratory. There are three known types of ordered polymers: parapolybenzothiazole; parapolybenzoxazole; and parapolybenzimidazole. The first has the greatest microwave-absorbency potential of the three.

Boeing has developed a thermoplastic material for its part in the advanced-technology fighter (ATF) program. The company built a full-scale, high-temperature resistant thermoplastic wing reinforced with graphite fibers to demonstrate advanced materials for possible use on Lockheed's YF-22 ATF. Boeing is responsible for manufacturing YF-22 primary and secondary structural members using thermoplastics. These parts will constitute 60 percent of the fighter's structural weight; total weight of the aircraft will be 20 percent lower than if conventional materials were used because of the thermoplastics.

Operationally the YF-22 aircraft will be easier to maintain because thermoplastics are tougher than thermoset composites and are easier to repair. Another advantage is that thermoplastics have thickness-to-weight ratios nearly three times smaller than those of other composite materials, so less material is needed to construct thermoplastic parts. As a result, there is more room for fuel tanks or avionics installations and total airframe weight *is reduced*.

Thermoplastic is graphite reinforced and can be layered in panels containing up to 60 plies. Unlike thermoset composites, thermoplastic materials and scrap can be reprocessed by being melted down at 380 degrees centigrade and reformed into new rigid parts. Compound curves, such as those needed in conformal engine air intakes and exhaust nozzles, are easily made using thermoplastics. Like thermoset composites, thermoplastic parts are cured at a high temperature and high pressure in an autoclave.

Although thermoset composites were once widely considered the wave of the future, production experience, according to the Air Force, has shown that they aren't as inexpensive as was once thought. The raw materials used to make thermoset composites are more expensive than expected, and manufacturing costs and scrap rates are high.

The advent of thermoplastics is resulting in new manufacturing processes, including automated hot-head tape-laying and postforming channels, that reduce times to build components to minutes instead of hours. Thermoplastics also can be stored indefinitely at room temperature, as opposed to thermoset composites, which require special environmentally controlled storage. The likely conclusion is that thermoplastics will be ideal for field repairs and easier to use in a factory setting than thermoset composites.

In addition to lower production costs, thermoplastics' ability to withstand higher temperatures means they will be well suited for construction of the supersonic—Mach 1.5—YF-22 ATF. Skin temperatures in certain areas of the ATF's airframe will reach as much as 175 degrees centigrade. This presents no problem for thermoplastic composites, but at those speeds and temperatures, a thermoset composite supersonic fighter would be useless because thermosets become unstable above 120 degrees centigrade.

Thermoplastics are more damage-resistant than thermoset composites, and any damage that occurs will be visible on the surface of the material. Thermoplastics will be used throughout the Lockheed YF-22, but metal will be used in areas where complex three-dimensional shapes and loading occur and, to ensure a wide margin of safety, where temperatures could rise above 175 degrees centigrade.

Thermoplastics are excellent radar-energy absorbers. They also can be made in such a way that they are transparent to radar energy.

Thermoset Composites. This material is made of high-strength carbon fibers embedded in an epoxy resin (FIG. 5-1). It is like Fiberglas, but uses carbon fibers instead of glass fibers. Thermoset composites have a higher strength-to-weight ratio than metals, but it costs one and a half times as much to manufacture parts from thermoset composites instead of aluminum. The material has a short shelf life and must be stored in controlled environment (freezers). The material is unstable above

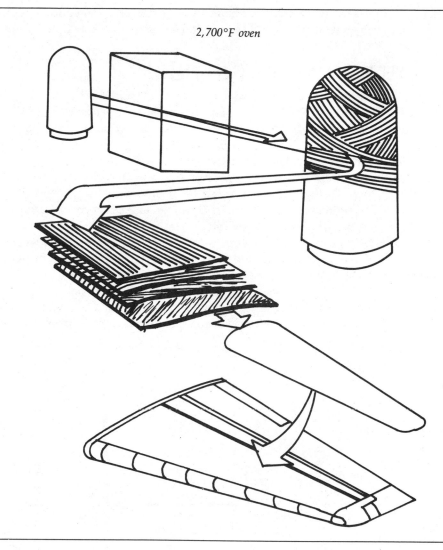

2,700°F oven

Fig. 5-1. Carbon fiber for parts made of composite materials is made from strands of polyacrylonitrile. The strands are oxidized at 2,700 degrees Fahrenheit, leaving 97 percent pure carbon fiber, which can be woven into various shapes. Shown is a unidirectional carbon-fiber weave which is impregnated with epoxy, cut, then layered in varying orientations to make, in this case, a wing panel.

120 degrees centigrade; however, Lockheed is evaluating high-temperature bismalemide resins for thermoset composites. Thermoset composite must be cured in an autoclave, under high temperature and pressure. Once cured, the material has undergone an irreversible chemical reaction, unlike thermoplastic composites, which can be cured, then reheated and reformed into new shapes.

Damage tolerance and toughness are problems occurring with thermoset composites. Although carbon fibers are inherently strong, they are embedded in a relatively weak and brittle resin. Impact damage on thermoset composites can cause internal structural damage that doesn't reveal itself externally, and sudden failures could occur to damaged parts with little visual notice that the material is near failure.

STEALTH PAINTS AND COATINGS

In Japan, a ferrite-based paint (iron oxide mixed with other metals in paint solution) was applied to five bridges. The paint is an effective radar-energy absorber, and radar operators on ships near the bridges can't see the bridges on their scopes, but can see other ships without the clutter from the bridges.

The U.S. Department of Defense has tried ferrite-based coatings on some aircraft, but although the paint did reduce the aircraft's radar signatures, the coating made the aircraft too heavy to fly, just as occurred with MX-410 in 1945. Research into effective and lightweight coatings continued, however, and advanced stealth paints are now being used for a variety of military vehicles, including ships, tanks, and aircraft (FIGS. 5-2 and 5-3). Any vehicle that is vulnerable to attack by radar-guided weapons is a candidate for stealth protection, and in the case of Army tanks, stealth camouflage nets as wells as paints are used to reduce radar signatures.

Iron Ball. One kind of stealth paint that has been somewhat successful in reducing RCS is known as iron ball. It is similar to ferrite-based paints, which are magnetic, but is lighter and more effective. Iron ball ranges in color from dull gray

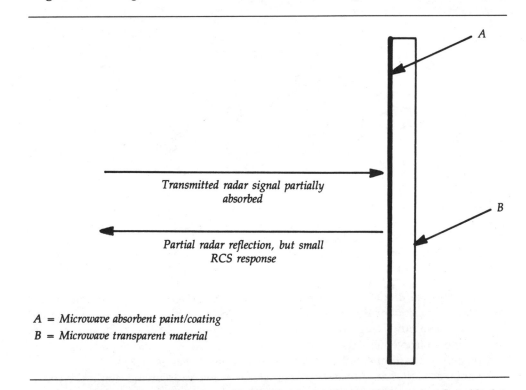

A = Microwave absorbent paint/coating
B = Microwave transparent material

Fig. 5-2. Incoming radar energy is partially absorbed by RAM paint. The rest is reflected back to the radar receiver, so this aircraft does not have such a low RCS.

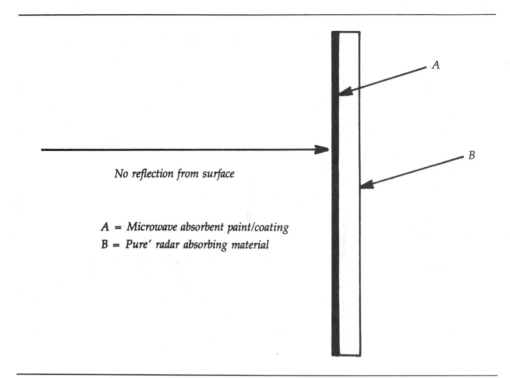

Fig. 5-3. Incoming radar energy is completely absorbed by the RAM paint and by the underlying RAM.

to flat black, and it not only absorbs radar energy, but also absorbs and dissipates infrared radiation (FIG. 5-4).

The paint's primary advantage is that its radar-energy distortion capability, or *mutability envelope*, can be manipulated through cockpit controls or automatic ECM equipment. By shifting the polarization of metal particles in the paint at ultrahigh frequencies and in irregular patterns, an aircraft coated with iron ball can distort radar reflections and confuse hostile radar operators with a great degree of success. Air traffic controllers will spot such an aircraft visually well before they can resolve it on their radar scopes, even though their radar is operating properly. If the pilot wishes his aircraft to be visible on the radar scope, he simply switches the polarity of the iron-ball coating so that the aircraft can be detected and tracked by radar.

Iron ball has been applied to Lockheed's TR-1 and SR-71 reconnaissance airplanes and to various RPVs. The SR-71's success at overflying communist territory without ever being intercepted is partially attributable to iron ball.

Retinyl Schiff Base Salt. This is a more recently developed RAM coating that reportedly reduces an aircraft's radar reflectivity by 80 percent. It is a nonferrous kind of stealth coating, and is black and looks like graphite. Retinyl Schiff base salts are polymers that contain double-bonded carbon-nitrogen structures linking divalent groups in the linear backbone of the molecule's polyene chain. Polarity is highly oriented in this material.

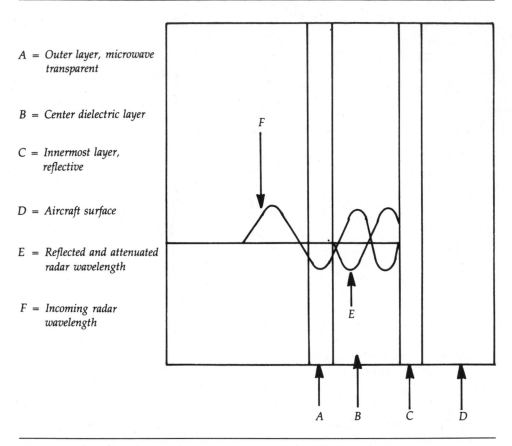

A = *Outer layer, microwave transparent*

B = *Center dielectric layer*

C = *Innermost layer, reflective*

D = *Aircraft surface*

E = *Reflected and attenuated radar wavelength*

F = *Incoming radar wavelength*

Fig. 5-4. A ferrite-based RAM coating such as iron ball usually consists of three layers. The inner surface of the outer layer (A) and the reflective inner layer (C) reflect radar energy, causing the incoming radar energy (F) and reflected radar energy (E) to cancel each other. The center dielectric layer (B) helps trap radar energy. Iron ball also absorbs and conducts infrared radiation evenly and smoothly and doesn't emit infrared radiation.

Radar-absorbing properties of retinyl Schiff base salt coatings are superior to other RAM coatings, and the coating weighs one-tenth as much as a typical ferrite-based coating like iron ball. Certain salts absorb specific wavelengths of radar energy. Scientists might be able to modify the salts so that a combination of salts could absorb the entire spectrum of radar energy, from long-wavelength, high-power radar to short-wavelength (millimeter wave) radar, and even frequencies used for bistatic radars. An aircraft coated with these modified salts could be virtually invisible to radar.

When radar energy is absorbed by these salts, the energy is dissipated as heat. The heat rejected by the salts' molecules is insignificant and would cause the temperature in the aircraft's skin to rise only a fraction of a degree.

These salts were developed by Robert Birge, director of the Center for Molecular Electronics at Carnegie-Mellon University in Pittsburgh, Pennsylvania. A chemical firm in Pennsylvania developed a suitable binder/resin that would accept these highly polarized salts.

A test of a coating containing these salts was conducted by the DOD in late 1987. The results remain classified. Carnegie-Mellon's Birge estimates that a coating, using the salts, could be produced in three years for about $3 million and would provide 80 percent radar-energy absorbency. With such a coating, Birge suggested, a fighter aircraft could be coated for about $30,000, making it possible to give nonstealth aircraft some stealth capability at modest cost.

LA1 Plessey Aerospace of Britain has developed a radar-absorbent material called **LA1**. This material comes in flat-plane tile form, and can be used in stealth construction (skins). LA1 material weighs about 0.6 pound/square foot.

MATERIALS FOR HEAT DISSIPATION AND NOISE REDUCTION

Synthetic materials containing substances such as carbon, boron, graphite, aramid, silicon, ceramic, and felt-metal are used to reduce infrared and noise signatures in stealth aircraft. These materials are used for internal linings in hot areas and for external noise-reducing skin coatings.

Gold and silver films can be added to internal portions of engine-bay cavities to reflect and dissipate engine heat, thus reducing the aircraft's infrared signature. Ultradense carbon-carbon foam absorbs and dissipates both radar energy and infrared radiation and is used in engine-bay cavities.

Outer surfaces of engines near exhaust pipes are coated with a ceramic-metal coating that dissipates heat rapidly and smoothly. This material has been used for many years and can be found on F-15s and other fighter aircraft. Not only does the ceramic coating reduce the fighter's infrared signature, but it retards corrosion and increases the life of parts to which it is applied.

Electric Wave Absorbing Material. A six-layer, nonwoven cloth made up of stainless steel and polyethyl fibers, developed by Nippon Electric Company (NEC) of Japan. This material can be applied to the inner walls of electronic bays within a stealth aircraft to eliminate electromagnetic leakage from the on-board avionic equipment, such as radars and communication and navigation systems. The material is claimed to eliminate up to 99 percent of emitted electromagnetic waves, including 4 to 14 GHz and 28 to 40 GHz.

Mesophase Pitch Fibers. An advanced composite material developed by Amoco, it has low-observable qualities that have shown to be far superior, in stiffness, to current materials. It also has three to five times the thermal conductivity to that of copper.

Chapter Six

Manned Aircraft with Some Stealth Technology

SEVERAL MANNED AIRCRAFT USE STEALTH TECHNOLOGY TO A SMALL EXtent. The following shows the names of these aircraft and their operational status. Details and specification on the aircraft follow.

Aircraft	Status
Lockheed U-2 Angel	Probably operational
Lockheed TR-1	Operational
Lockheed SR-71 Blackbird	Operational
Lockheed QT-2 Prize Crew	No longer operational
Lockheed Q-Star	Test only
Lockheed YO-3	No longer operational
Lockheed QU-22B Pave Eagle	No longer operational
Windecker YE-5	Test only
Wren Quiet Bird	Operational
Rockwell B-1B	Operational

LOCKHEED U-2 ANGEL

After the Soviet Union exploded its first hydrogen bomb in August 1953 and began developing strategic bombers like the Bear, Bison, and Badger, the U.S. Air Force began PROJECT BALD EAGLE. Even though there was little stealth technology at the time, the program specified an aircraft that could fly high enough to be well out of range of known antiaircraft defenses. Such capability would enable the aircraft to overfly Soviet territory with little risk of being shot down, even by radar-directed antiaircraft guns.

Bell offered to fulfill the requirements of the BALD EAGLE program with its X-16 reconnaissance aircraft (FIG. 6-1). Range of the X-16 would be about 3,000 nautical

Fig. 6-1. Bell's X-16 was proposed for the Air Force's Bald Eagle program in 1953, but lost the contract to Lockheed's U-2. (Courtesy Bell Aerospace TEXTRON)

miles at 65,000 feet or higher. It had an extremely thin fuselage and a long-span wing with an aspect ratio of about 12:1. Two wing-mounted nonafterburning Pratt & Whitney J57 turbojets were reportedly the powerplants slated for the X-16. At 72,000 feet, the X-16's cruise speed was estimated at Mach 0.75, carrying a payload of target analysis equipment and search cameras.

Rollout of the aircraft was to have occurred only 18 months after signing of the contract, but in 1955, after a year's work on the project, the Air Force canceled the X-16. The X-16 was a secret for nearly 20 years, until a U.S. government employee who had worked on the project revealed details of the X-16 program at a meeting in 1975 in Washington, D.C.

Lockheed's famous Skunkworks—the company's Advanced Projects Development Division headed by Clarence "Kelley" Johnson—also had an airplane to offer the Air Force for the BALD EAGLE Program. Lockheed proposed a modified F-104 jet having wings with a high-aspect ratio, and powered by a single Pratt & Whitney J57 turbojet engine. Johnson refined the design and convinced the Air Force and CIA to sign a contract with Lockheed for what eventually became the famous U-2 reconnaissance aircraft, shown in FIG. 6-2. (The U stands for utility; it was probably an attempt by the CIA to conceal the purpose of the aircraft.) The contract was signed in late 1954.

Johnson and fifty hand-picked engineers worked around the clock at Lockheed's Palmdale, California, plant on what Lockheed termed PROJECT AQUATONE. Lockheed's designation for the U-2 was Model CL-282. The first U-2 was designed and built under heavy secrecy (and at Lockheed's expense) at the Palmdale facility and trucked in sections to the Ranch Airstrip (now known as Watertown Strip near Groom Dry Lake, Nevada). After assembly at Ranch Airstrip, the U-2 made its first flight on August 6, 1955, piloted by Lockheed Test Pilot Tony LeVier. Only eight months had passed since signing of the initial contract.

CIA and Air Force pilots immediately began training in the U-2, and shortly thereafter began making clandestine flights near Soviet borders and over Soviet territory. The purpose of the flights was to gather intelligence data that would either confirm or deny a Soviet military buildup. Most operational U-2 flights were made without any visible markings on the aircraft; the U-2s were usually painted flat black— an early form of RAM—to mask the aircraft against the black-sky background typical of the altitudes at which they were flown. When the public first got a glimpse of the

Fig. 6-2. The Lockheed U-2 high-altitude reconnaissance aircraft. (Courtesy Lockheed-California Co.)

U-2, it was marked with civil or National Advisory Committee on Aeronautics (NACA, now NASA) registration numbers.

Weight-saving design techniques helped the U-2 achieve its efficient high-altitude performance. An example is the U-2's bicycle-style landing gear, similar to the single wheel mounted on the belly of a sailplane. With external wing-mounted slipper fuel tanks, the U-2 could fly up to 4,000 miles at a cruise speed of 460 miles per hour. The U-2's fuel consumption is reportedly about 5 miles per gallon, an incredibly high number for a turbine-powered aircraft.

Until Gary Powers was shot down by a Soviet SA-2 surface-to-air missile while flying a U-2 over Soviet territory in May 1960, the U-2 had been used for intelligence-gathering missions with near total immunity from hostile defenses. Photographs taken during these early overflights confirmed that the Soviets did not have the large missile or bomber forces that had been reported by U.S. DOD officials.

As Soviet air defenses improved in the late 1950s and early 1960s, the U-2 no longer enjoyed its former immunity. Early versions of the U-2 used some form of RAM, but its effectiveness has not been revealed. The nonafterburning turbojet engine contributed to infrared signature suppression, as did the boost-glide flight profile used on U-2 missions. Over hostile territory, the U-2 pilot would climb to the aircraft's maximum altitude, then shut the engine down, glide to a lower altitude, and start the engine again. This technique saved fuel—the U-2 is not refuelable in flight—and helped make the U-2 difficult to detect the tract. With its high aspect-ratio wings, very little engine power was needed to keep the U-2 aloft over hostile territory; hence, the U-2's small infrared signature.

Detection technology outpaced the U-2 and when it became obvious that the U-2 was vulnerable to hostile attack, the CIA and Air Force asked the aerospace industry to design a successor. This requirement eventually became the Mach 3-plus Lockheed A-12/SR-71 Series aircraft.

U-2s were flown, not only over Soviet territory, but also over China, Cuba, Veitnam, and many other nations. Foreign pilots have flown U-2s; Taiwan Air Force pilots flew U-2s over China for the CIA. U-2s are still in the active inventory of the CIA and Air Force and are probably still being flown on convert missions.

Many versions of the U-2 were built, including the U-2A through U-2J, U2-CT, U-2EPX, and U-2R. Most U-2s were single-seat types, except the U-2CT and U-2D, which had two fore and aft seats with the second seat raised slightly above the forward seat. During its career, the U-2 has picked up a few nicknames and code names, two of which are "Black Angel" and "Dragon Lady."

U-2 Specifications

Length	50 ft (early versions)
	60 ft plus (later versions)
Wingspan	80 ft (early versions)
	103 ft (U-2R)
Height	16 ft, 1 in (U-2R)
Wing area	565 sq ft (early versions)
	1,000 sq ft (U-2R)

Empty weight	9,920 to 11,700 lb
	(early versions)
	14,990 lb (U2-R)
Takeoff weight	14,800 lb (U-2A)
	16,000 lb (U-2B/C/CT/D, 17,270
	lb with wing tanks)
	41,000 lb (U-2R)
Wing loading	26.2 to 30.6 lb/sq ft
	(early versions)
	41.0 lb/sq ft (U-2R)
Power loading	19.8 lb/sq ft (U-2A/B)
	17.0 lb/sq ft (U-2R)
Maximum speed	494 mph (U-2A)
	528 mph (U-2B/C/CT/D)
	510 mph (U-2R)
Cruise speed	460 mph
Operational altitude	70,000 ft (U-2A)
	85,000 ft (U-2B/C/CT/D)
	90,000 ft (U-2R)
Maximum range	2,200 mi (U-2A)
	3,000 mi (U-2B/C/CT/D)
	3,500 mi (U-2R)
	(increase with external fuel)
Powerplant	P&W J57-P-37A, 11,200 lb (U-2A)
	P&W J75-P-13A, 15,000 lb (U-2C)
	P&W J75-P-13B, 17,000 lb (U-2R
	and later versions of U-2C)

LOCKHEED TR-1

An out-of-production aircraft was resurrected by the U.S. Air Force for the first time when it signed a contract with Lockheed in 1979 for the TR-1 (FIG. 6-3). TR stands for tactical reconnaissance, and the TR-1 is a version of the U-2R, production of which ended in 1968. Both the TR-1 and U-2R are about 40 percent larger than the original U-2 and were designed by Lockheed's Clarence Johnson. The TR-1 was ordered to meet the requirements left vacant by the canceled Boeing YQM-94A Compass Cope B-Gull unmanned air vehicle.

The all-aluminum TR-1 is powered by the same engine found in the U2-R, Pratt & Whitney's 17,000-lb J75-P-13B turbojet. The airframe is coated with flat-black iron ball RAM and has small, red low-visibility markings. Various nose sections, mission-bay hatches, and wing pods can be mounted on the TR-1, depending on the mission, and up to 2 tons of sensors and experiment packages can be carried. The TR-1 pilot wears a pressure suit—like a space suit—and the cockpit has a food warmer to heat food in tubes like those used in space missions. Avionics suite includes HF, UHF, and VHF comm radios, and GPS, TACAN, and ADF nav radios.

Fig. 6-3. The Lockheed/Air Force TR-1 tactical long-endurance surveillance aircraft. (Courtesy Lockheed-California Co.)

Mission-specific equipment includes an advanced synthetic-aperture radar system called UPD-X SLAR (side-looking airborne radar), ECM equipment, and a secure digital datalink. With SLAR, the TR-1 can ''see'' deep inside hostile territory (at oblique angles) without having to overfly the territory. The range of SLAR is about 35 miles. Some TR-1s are expected to be equipped with the (precision-location strike system (PLSS).

The Air Force contract with Lockheed called for 20 single-seat TR-1s and two TR-1B two-seat conversion trainers. Twelve TR-1As are assigned to RAFB Alconbury in the United Kingdom, and have been operated by Air Force Strategic Air Command crews on behalf of U.S. Air Forces in Europe (USAFE) since 1982. Beale AFB, north of Sacramento, California, is the primary American TR-1 base.

TR-1 variants include the TR-1A, TR-1B, and a type that appeared in 1984 with a large airfoil-shaped radome that presumably houses some type of early-warning radar. The PLSS-equipped TR-1A has a slightly bulged nose section where the equipment is mounted. NASA's ER-2 is basically a TR-1; it is used to fly earth-resources missions for NASA from the agency's Ames Research Center of Moffet Naval Air Station in Mountain View, California.

The TR-1's high aspect-ratio wings—long span and short chord—enable the aircraft to fly to extremely high altitudes. Outrigger wheels on the wingtips steady the TR-1 as it takes off on its bicycle-style landing gear. The tip wheels drop off when the TR-1 leaves the runway. On landing, wingtip-mounted skids keep the wings from being damaged when they scrape on the runway.

TR-1s can provide all-weather, day or night battlefield surveillance to support American and allied ground and air forces. The aircraft can be used to identify hostile targets and threats that are well behind enemy lines without needing to penetrate hostile airspace. The TR-1's sensor suite can include advanced infrared systems and electronic intelligence (Elint) devices.

TR-1 Specifications

Length   63 ft
Maximum endurance   12 hr
All other specifications similar to the U-2R.

LOCKHEED SR-71 BLACKBIRD

Although it is not normally considered a stealth aircraft, the SR-71 (FIG. 6-4) is one of few aircraft that have been designed from the beginning with stealth technology. Clarence Johnson had a major influence on the design of the SR-71, which took shape in Lockheed's famed Skunkworks.

Several versions of this Mach 3-plus aircraft have been built. They include the single-seat A-12; the two-seat A-12: the two-seat A-12 reconnaissance type (sometimes called the M-12), which carried a Lockheed D-21 Mach 4 drone; the never-built R-12

Fig. 6-4. The Lockheed/Air Force SR-71 Blackbird Mach 3 reconnaissance aircraft. (Courtesy Lockheed-California Co.)

bomber version; the YF-12A two-seat interceptor prototype; the F-12B, a proposed service version of the YF-12A; the YF-12C, used by NASA; the SR-71 reconnaissance type; and the SR-71B/C two-seat trainer.

The SR-71 is the result of several CIA-sponsored studies conducted by a number of aerospace companies in the late 1950s. Boeing, North American (now Rockwell International), General Dynamics, and Lockheed all presented proposals to the CIA in 1958 and 1959. The requirement was for a replacement for the U-2 that was capable of flying between Mach 3 and Mach 4 at 80,000 feet or higher. The CIA considered both the proposals from General Dynamics and Lockheed acceptable.

General Dynamics proposed several aircraft that it felt could meet the CIA's requirements and named its version "Fish" or "Kingfish." One type was small enough to be launched by a modified B-58 bomber. Another type featured an oval-shaped delta-wing planform. A two-stage vehicle was proposed, with the part intended to overfly hostile territory to be made of ceramic radar-absorbent and heat-resistant materials.

Lockheed won the contract and General Dynamics's radical designs never made it off the drawing board. Earlier Lockheed studies for a Mach 3 aircraft centered around a large hydrogen-fueled aircraft with the Lockheed model number L-400. Lockheed's final proposal, and the one that was accepted by the CIA in August 1959, was for the single-seat A-12. Workers at the Skunkworks referred to it as the "Thing," while the CIA designation was OXCART and ROADRUNNER. The A-12's first flight was on April 26, 1962, from Watertown Strip, where the craft had been assembled.

The A-12 first flew with two afterburning P&W J75 turbojet engines, but the P&W turbo-ramjet engine became and still is the SR-71 Blackbird's standard engine.

Because of the extreme aerodynamic heating experienced by the A-12 when flying at more than Mach 3 and the subsequent expansion of the metal in the airframe, much of its structure is made of strong titanium. A side benefit of the aerodynamic heating is that each time the Blackbird flies at top speed, the titanium receives an extra heat treatment, thus helping the structure maintain its high strength.

RCS reduction was a primary goal for the SR-71's airframe, and that is why the Blackbird has such a unique shape. The dual vertical fins are canted inward for low RCS, and the double delta-wing, flat-bottom fuselage planform with chin strakes that terminate at the nose radome contributes greatly to the SR-71's low RCS. Wing leading edges, chin strakes, and vertical-fin leading edges consist of Lockheed-designed titanium-backed triangular structures with internal plastic inserts that absorb radar energy (see FIG. 4-6). Many special materials and coatings developed by Lockheed are applied to the SR-71, and the aircraft is painted with infrared- and radar energy-absorbing iron ball.

Iron ball's fuel resistence is an added advantage for the SR-71 because while at rest, the aircraft's fuel tanks leak. The SR-71 expands so much at high speeds that when the airframe is cool, there are many ill-fitting parts in the airframe, especially near the fuel tanks. As the airframe expands from aerodynamic heating, the parts fit together better and the leaks stop until the SR-71 lands.

Twenty percent of the SR-71's external surfaces are made of heat-resistant ceramic plastics, and if this material should be exposed to leaking fuel, it could cause an explosion when the airframe heats up to more than 600 degrees Fahrenheit. The

SR-71 frequently experiences higher temperatures than that, so it is important that the ceramic plastics be well protected. These plastics are also used on external areas of the SR-71's reconnaissance systems, such as camera apertures and radomes. An advanced ECM/ECCM/ESM (electronic countermeasures, counter-countermeasures, and support measures) suite is installed in the SR-71 and contributes to the low observability of the aircraft.

The SR-71 pilot and reconnaissance systems officer sit in tandem, in individual pressurized cockpits, and each wears a pressure suit similar to that worn by space shuttle astronauts. Range of the aircraft can be extended by aerial refueling from KC-135Q and KC-10A tankers modified to carry the SR-71's special JP7 fuel.

The first operational version was the A-12, the highest and fastest flying of the series. USAF and CIA pilots made numerous flights in A-12s over highly sensitive areas, but everyone involved was able to keep the A-12 under wraps for nearly 20 years before its existence was disclosed to the public. Another version of the aircraft was revealed to the public in 1964, however, when the USAF requested an intercepter version of the A-12, called the YF-12A. This request was actually a CIA-sponsored cover for secret operation of the A-12. The YF-12A was supposed to be a replacement for the canceled North American F-108 Rapier Mach 3 interceptor. Ironically, when the F-108 was canceled in 1959, the first contracts for the A-12 were signed.

The service version of the YF-12A was to be called the F-12B and carry four to eight 100-mile-range air-to-air missiles with nuclear warheads. Bother the radar and the Hughes missile system of the YF-12A/F12B were adapted from the proposed F-108 interceptor.

Another version, called the R-12, was to be a bomber armed with nuclear weapons carried in three fuselage weapons bays. However, this version was never built.

It has been reported from bases where SR-71s are deployed on temporary duty (TDY) that air traffic controllers are frequently unable to detect the SR-71 on their radar scopes. The controllers apparently are able to spot the SR-71 visually before seeing it on their scopes. The SR-71's application of stealth technology is so effective that it probably requires some sort of transponder or beacon so that friendly forces can detect it on their radars, otherwise it won't show up on the screens.

At some TDY bases, SR-71s reportedly are stored in underground hangars. The hangars are said to have elevators, and when an SR-71 lands, it is quickly guided to the elevator and dropped down to its underground hangar, out of sight of any prying eyes. The underground hangars are located in secluded areas of foreign bases where SR-71s are deployed.

One source said that he once saw an SR-71 land at a TDY base. He briefly turned away, and when he looked back where the SR-71 had been, it was gone. He asked another person who had also seen the SR-71 land where it went, and he was quickly reminded that it would be best not to openly admit that he had seen an SR-71 because, offically, the SR-71 was not deployed at that base. It is likely that the SR-71 seen by the source was on a covert mission of great sensitivity.

With the low infrared and low RCS of the SR-71, there is one other special feature of the aircraft that has gained little attention in the open press: its unique reconnaissance camera apertures (windows).

These apertures are different from other known systems. The SR-71's cameras must obtain the clearest and sharpest photographs of its subject at speeds of Mach 3-plus and altitudes above 90,000 feet. With such flight conditions, the skin temperatures, especially around the camera apertures, would create aberancies in ordinary aircraft transparencies that might otherwise distort the images on the required photographs to an unacceptable level.

Lockheed engineers, in cooperation with other industries, have developed a high-temperature-resistant ceramic/plastic that is totally opaque at low speeds, but that turns completely transparent above Mach 2.6 and does not cause any distortion of the images of the camera systems on the SR-71. These ceramic material apertures appear on the bottom of the SR-71's chin areas forward, and appear as white patches in photographs.

A-12/SR-71 Specifications

Length	98 ft, 9 in (A-12)
	101 ft, 8 in (YF-12)
	103 ft, 10 in (SR-71)
Wingspan	55 ft, 7 in
Height	18 ft, 3 in (A-12/YF-12)
	18 ft, 6 in (SR-71)
Empty weight	60,000 lb (A-12)
	60,730 lb (YF-12)
	67,500 lb (SR-71)
Maximum takeoff weight	120,000 lb (A-12)
	127,000 lb (YF-12)
	172,000 lb (SR-71)
Maximum speed	Mach 3.6 (A-12)
	Mach 3.35 (operational for YF-12/SR-71)
Operating altitude	95,000 ft (A-12)
	85,000 ft (YF-12/SR71) (Some reports state that all versions can fly up to 125,000 ft)
Maximum range (without refueling)	2,500 mi (A-12/YF-12)
	3,250 mi (SR-71) P&W J75 afterburning, 26,000 lb (used on first A-12s) P&W J58 afterburning, turbo-ramjet 32,500 lb, 15% higher @ Mach 3 (subsequent A-12s and all other versions)

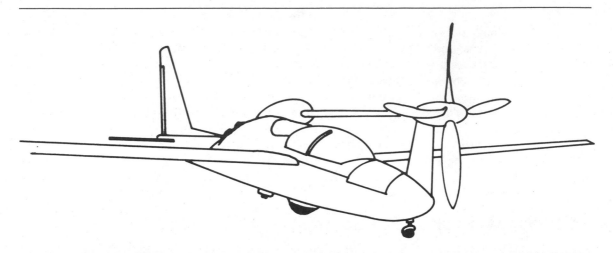

Fig. 6-5. The Lockheed QT-2PC Prize Crew quiet reconnaissance aircraft.

Fig. 6-6. Schweizer SA 2-37 special-purpose aircraft. This is a quiet aircraft with long endurance and a very small infrared signature designed to meet special civil or military requirements. It is similar to Lockheed's YO-3A quiet reconnaissance aircraft; in fact, both the YO-3A and SA 2-37 are modified versions of Schweizer's SGS 2-32 sailplane. (Courtesy Schewizer Aircraft)

LOCKHEED QT-2 QUIET THRUSTER

The QT-2 (FIG. 6-5) was designed by Lockheed as a quiet reconnaissance aircraft. Funded by DARPA though the U.S. Army, the first QT-2 flew in August 1967. Two QT-2s were fitted with night optical sensors and underwent operational evaluation in Vietnam. QT-2s tested in Vietnam during the Tet Offensive reportedly made reconnaissance flights as low as 100 feet without being detected by hostile forces. The noise emitted by the QT-2's engine and propeller is said to be similar to the sound of wind blowing through trees.

The QT-2's airframe is based on that of a Schweizer SGS 2-32 sailplane (FIG. 6-6). The engine is buried in the fuselage behind the cockpit and drives a prop shaft over the cockpit to the nose-mounted propeller. A silencer-suppressor type of muffler keeps the engine's noise to a minimum, and the four-blade wood prop is extremely quiet as a result of its slow speed and large diameter. Landing gear is the bicycle style with a large main wheel on the aircraft's belly and an additional small wheel on the nose. The QT-2 carries one pilot and one sensor/equipment operator sitting in tandem under a one-piece canopy. The design was later refined into the QT-2PC Prize Crew version. The QT-2PCs were passed on to the U.S. Navy for use as trainers. The designation changed to X-26A/B.

LOCKHEED Q-STAR (QUIET STAR)

The Q-Star (FIG. 6-7) was a private venture by Lockheed designed to improve the acoustic signature reduction systems of the QT-2. The first Q-Star flew in June 1968. It also used the airframe of Schweizer's SGS 2-32 sailplane, but the airframe was more extensively modified then on the QT-2. The wingspan was extended and stronger spars and thicker wing skins were added. Seven square feet were added to the area of the empennage, and conventional main and tailwheel landing gear were installed. The tailwheel is steerable and brakes are fitted on the main gear.

The engine and propeller arrangement is similar to the QT-2. The first engine was 100-hp Continental 0-200-A, but after some testing, Lockheed replaced that with a quieter Curtiss-Wright RC 2-60 rotary engine derated to 185 horsepower. The rotary engine, according to Lockheed, has a better power-to-weight ratio and is inherently quieter than conventional piston engines.

The RC 2-60 is liquid cooled, and cooling of the fluid is accomplished by an automobile-style radiator installed in a box-like structure in the nose below the propeller shaft. Exhaust noise is reduced by a three-chamber silencer consisting of two large chambers and one smaller chamber between the large chambers. The exhaust tailpipe points upward.

The engine is mounted behind the cockpit, as on the QT-2, and drives a long propeller shaft through a two-stage V-belt reduction system. The reduction ratio is 4.34 : 1. The propeller shaft, which passes over the cockpit, is supported by a 3-foot pylon mounted on the nose of the aircraft. With such a large reduction ratio, the prop, which is over 7 feet in diameter, turns very slowly at a paltry 500 revolutions per minute. Props ranging in diameter from 7.5 feet to 8.3 feet were tested, as were some with three, four, and six blades.

Fig. 6-7. *The Lockheed Q-Star experimental quiet research aircraft.* (Courtesy Lockheed-California Co.)

Q-Star Specifications

Length	31 ft
Wingspan	57 ft, 1 in
Horizontal stabilizer span	10 ft, 6 in
Empty weight, equipped	2,166 lb

LOCKHEED YO-3

The YO-3 (Fig. 6-8) is a quiet reconnaissance aircraft derived from Lockheed's QT-2 and Q-Star series. Lockheed signed the initial $2 million YO-3 contract in 1968.

The Schweizer SGS 2-32 sailplane formed the foundation for the YO-3, except the YO-3 is a low-wing configuration with the wing roots wider to accommodate retractable main landing gear. The YO-3 also has a tailwheel, but it is larger than that of the Q-Star. Extensive modifications to the fuselage resulted in crew seats farther to the rear under a much larger canopy. The YO-3's pilot seat is the rearmost seat.

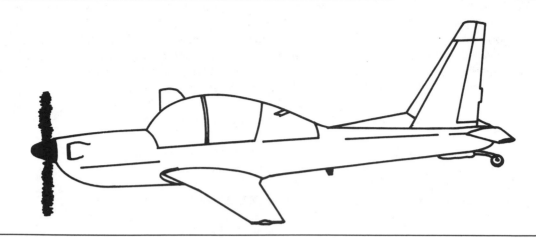

Fig. 6-8. The Lockhead YO-3A quiet reconnaissance aircraft.

A 210-hp six-cylinder Continental piston engine was mounted directly in the nose this time, avoiding the need for complex, long prop shafts. Early YO-3s had six-blade wood propellers, but these were eventually replaced by three-blade constant-speed propellers.

YO-3s were equipped with infrared sensors and other optical night-sensor systems and have been operated by the U.S. Army, CIA, and NASA. The aircraft was deployed in Vietnam for one year, and on reconnaissance missions the YO-3 proved valuable for gathering information on nighttime enemy troop movements.

Schweizer later designed an aircraft with similar appearance and performance as the YO-3, called the SA 2-37A. The main difference was that the SA 2-37A had side-by-side seating, instead of tandem seating.

YO-3 Specifications

Length	30 ft
Wingspan	57 ft
Operating speed range	58 to 138 mph
Quietest speed	70 mph
Endurance	6.0 hr
First deployed	Vietnam 1970; no weapons

BEECH AIRCRAFT QU-22B PAVE EAGLE

Under U.S. Air Force contract, Sperry-Rand modified a civil Beech A36 Bonanza for use as a reconnaissance aircraft. The modified aircraft, called the QU-22B, operated from bases in Thailand during the Vietnam War in the 1960s. Its mission was reconnaissance and surveillance of enemy troop infiltration into South Vietnam.

The QU-22B could be flown either manned or as an unmanned drone. Most missions in Vietnam were conducted with just one pilot on board. QU-22B specifications that are different from the civil A36's include: Continental GTSIO-520 reduction-geared engine, instead of the normal TSIO-520 Continental without reduction gearing thus allowing the large-diameter three-bladed Hartzell propeller to turn much more slowly and quietly; a larger output 28V alternator, plus a second belt-driven alternator installed above the propeller reduction-gear housing; an extended wingspan; tip fuel tanks; and no rear cabin windows (which were installed on the civilian A36).

External surfaces of the QU-22B airframe sported a number of antennae for Elint equipment provided by Radiation Inc. On-board electronic equipment was installed where the rear seats normally are on the A36.

Specifications are similar to the civil A36, but the QU-22B has a 5,200-lb maximum takeoff weight.

WINDECKER INDUSTRIES YE-5

Dr. Leo Windecker approached the U.S. Air Force in 1963 with a proposal for an aircraft with a low RCS, but nothing resulted from those meetings. In 1973, after Windecker built a prototype composite aircraft, called the AC-7 Eagle 1, on his own, the Air Force expressed a renewed interest in low-RCS designs and reopened discussions with Windecker. The result was that Windecker lent his prototype Eagle to the Air Force for research into low-RCS technology.

During testing of the Eagle (military designation YE-5), the Air Force found that the aircraft had an unacceptably high RCS because of the metal used to support the structure internally. The Air Force gave Windecker a contract to build an aircraft that would adhere more completely to stealth philosophy through RCS-reducing airframe shape and more use of RAM, and this became the YE-5A. It was first tested by the Air Force, then by the Army, and also by Lockheed. These tests were all highly classified.

Windecker did achieve FAA certification of his Fiberglas Eagle, and built a few of the type, but the aircraft never went into production. The Eagle was notable because it was a pioneer in composite construction techniques and received certification many years before the current crop of composite airplanes.

WREN AIRCRAFT QUIET BIRD

The Quiet Bird is an Air Force version of the Wren 460P STOL modification of Cessna Aircraft Co.'s four-seat 182 light single-engine aircraft. Noise and infrared suppressors and decoys have been added to reduce the Quiet Bird's detectability. It also might have a light coat of RAM paint on most external surfaces. Much of the airframe is made of radar-transparent materials.

The external configuration is similar to the civil version—high wing, nose-mounted engine, tricycle landing gear, conventional empennage—except for installation of classified military equipment. Missions for the Quiet Bird are thought to include covert

Elint, with infrared optics used to detect troop or vehicle movements in darkness. An obvious physical feature of the Quiet Bird is the large pod under the starboard wing, which most likely contains sophisticated electronic equipment.

The Quiet Bird can operate from very short airstrips and is reportedly being used in Central America. Probable crew size is three to four persons, including the pilot.

Quiet Bird Specifications

Length	27 ft, 4 in
Wingspan	35 ft, 10 in
Height	9 ft
Maximum takeoff weight	3,650 lb
Maximum speed	160 mph
Economy cruise speed	140 mph
Stall speed	29 mph
Surveillance speed	50 mph
Takeoff and landing distance	270 ft
Range	980 mi
Powerplant	230-hp Continental 0-470 modified with noise and infrared suppressers

ROCKWELL INTERNATIONAL B-1B BOMBER

The B-1 bomber is not officially part of U.S. military "black" programs, but both the B-1A and B-1B were designed to incorporate low-observable technology, and both would present a difficult target for hostile air defenses. Design features of the B-1A (FIG. 6-9) give it a markedly lower RCS than the B-52 it was designed to replace. Refinements on the B-1B (FIG. 6-10), including RAM added to certain areas and

Fig. 6-9. Rockwell International/Air Force B-1A bomber prototype. (Courtesy U.S. Air Force)

Fig. 6-10. Rockwell International/Air Force B-1B variable geometry wing strategic bomber operated by the strategic Air Command. (Courtesy Rockwell International)

redesigned portions of the internal structure, have reduced the B-1B's detectability signature by ten times compared to the B-1A.

Newly designed engine intakes direct airflow to the engines in a snake-like pattern. Intake ducts have radar-absorbing baffles that capture radar energy, preventing it from reflecting back to hostile radar receivers. Engine pods have infrared-dissipating properties that, along with infrared jammers mounted between the engines' exhaust nozzles, reduce the aircraft's infrared signature.

The B-1B is a medium-weight bomber designed as a strategic penetrator and is intended to modernize the SAC fleet. Although President Carter canceled the B-1A program on June 30, 1977, he did allow testing and development of the bomber to continue. In 1981, President Reagan reinstated the B-1 program and eventually 100 B-1Bs were ordered. Final deliveries took place in mid-1988.

Modifications made to the B-1B design that make it different from the B-1A include: increased maximum takeoff weight; seperate ejection seats for each member of the four-man crew; fixed air intake inlets; redesigned engine pods with a simplified overwing fairing; and reduced infrared and radar signature. The modifications improve mission success probability when the B-1B is operating at low levels.

The B-1B's terrain-following radar, a Westinghouse AN/APQ-164 multipurpose offensive system, is a modified version of the radar used in the F-16 fighter. The radar has frequency agility, Doppler-beam sharpening, and stealth features in the radar itself, either in its positioning in the radome or different modes of operation. The nose radome has been modified to have several flat-sided areas and is made of special dielectric ceramics that are radar transparent. The radar antenna is a phased-array type, with fixed pitch-scan, but movable in azimuth.

The pilot and copilot sit in the front cockpit, and the defensive and offensive systems operators occupy the rear cockpits. View ports are installed in the systems operators' cockpits. The possibility of nuclear attack has been taken into account in the B-1B design, and the aircraft is nuclear hardened. The cockpits have nuclear-flash protection for the crew, and the avionics are hardened against nuclear electromagnetic pulse. Crew access is through a retractable ladder behind the nose gear. Landing gear is the tricycle style with four wheels on each main gear and two wheels on the nose gear.

The B-1B's variable-geometry wing (swing wing) enables the aircraft to fly efficiently at supersonic speeds with the wings swept back, but also to take off and land on relatively short runways with the wings extended to provide additional life for low-speed operations. B-1A test aircraft have reached top speeds of Mach 2.2, flown above 50,000 ft, demonstrated manual and automatic terrain following at Mach 0.85 below 200 feet, dropped a variety of ordnance loads, and completed a number of tests designed to verify the version's capabilities in combat environments.

B-1B testing is still active and will continue. Deployment is planned as follows: Dyess AFB, Texas, 29; Ellsworth AFB, South Dakota, 35; Grand Forks AFB, North Dakota, 17; and McConnell AFB, Kansas, 17. Two B-1Bs will be permanently stationed at Edwards AFB in California for the testing and development program. The 100th, and final, B-1B was delivered to the U.S. Air Force in mid-1988.

The first B-1A flew December 23, 1974, from Palmdale, California, to Edwards AFB. Four prototype B-1As were built before the program was canceled in 1977. The first flight of the B-1B was on October 18, 1984.

B-1B Bomber Specifications

Length	151 ft
Wingspan	137 ft swept forward
	78 ft swept aft
Height	34 ft
Maximum takeoff weight	477,000 lb
Weapons payload	75,000 lb internal weapons in three bays 50,000 lb external on 14 semi-conformal weapon/fuel pylons. [Common strategic rotary launcher mounted internally.

Maximum speed	Mach 1.6 at high altitude
	Mach 0.95 at low altitude
Range (without refueling)	5,000-plus mi
Powerplant	Four 30,000-lb GE F101-GE-102 turbofan engines
Weapons	All conventional munitions, nuclear warheads, ALCM, ACM, SRAM I and II, Harpoon

Chapter Seven

Manned Aircraft Pure Stealth Design

THESE AIRCRAFT IN THIS CHAPTER HAVE BEEN DESIGNED FROM THE ground up to be pure stealth aircraft, capable of remaining undetected by hostile forces while operating in hostile territory. Operational status of these aircraft is listed, followed by details and specifications.

Manned Stealth Aircraft	*Status*
Lockheed F-117A	Operational
Lockheed/Air Force Aurora hypersonic stealth reconnaissance aircraft	Operational
Northrop/Air Force B-2 ATB	IOC* 1990
Northrop/Air Force tactical stealth aircraft	Testing
McDonnell Douglas/General Dynamics A-12 ATA	Under development
General Dynamics Model-100	Under development or possibly testing
Air Force YF-22, YF-23 ATF	Under development

*Initial operational capability

LOCKHEED/AIR FORCE F-117A

The U.S. Air Force designated this program CSIRS (Covert Survivable In-weather Reconnaissance/Strike), and it is a key part of highly classified American "black" programs generically labeled *low-observable technology*. To the public, the F-117A is the aircraft that generates images of miraculous fighters almost invisible to the eye that can come and go as they please, and are undetectable by radars that constantly monitor potential aggressors. The facts that are known about these black programs show that there is more than a little truth in the public perception of the characteristics of the fighters and bombers that will equip many front-line Air Force and Navy squadrons by the year 2000.

Research that led to development of the F-117A originated with a series of studies contracted by the U.S. Air Force and DARPA in early 1973, code-named HAVE BLUE. In the same year, the Air Force began testing the Fiberglas Windecker Eagle to see how much the airplane's composite materials contributed to RCS reduction. Modifications made to the Eagle to further reduce its RCS—having to do with the contribution of shape to RCS reduction—indicated the direction research should take in the HAVE BLUE program.

By the end of 1973, the HAVE BLUE studies had produced enough results that the Air Force decided to invite proposals from the aerospace industry for construction of technology demonstrator prototype aircraft. The program was renamed XST (Experimental Stealth Tactical) and was partially funded by DARPA.

XST program goals were for an aircraft with the following attributes: very low RCS, particularly head-on; extensive use of RAM, both for exterior skins and interior structural parts; airframe shaped for reduced RCS; minimized engine noise and cooled exhaust to reduce acoustic and infrared signature; ability to carry advanced ECM/ECCM/ESM equipment; and reduced visual signature so that it would be difficult to see from a few hundred yards.

Boeing, Grumman, LTV, Lockheed, McDonnell Douglas, and Northrop all responded to the Air Force/DARPA XST request for proposals in late 1975. Lockheed and Northrop were finalists, and each built a flying scaled-down prototype for a competitive fly-off. In 1976, Lockheed won the production contract for what the Air Force still calls the CSIRS program.

The security surrounding the HAVE BLUE program was relaxed briefly when the media announced that Lockheed would be building a stealth fighter. As it had in the past with the U-2 and SR-71, Lockheed assigned the project to its Skunkworks and called Clarence ''Kelly'' Johnson out of retirement to take charge of the project in a consultant capacity.

A number of flying and nonflying scaled-down prototypes of stealth aircraft were tested in Lockheed's wind tunnels and anechoic microwave test chambers. Just over a year after signing the contract, Lockheed's proof-of-concept XST prototype was shipped from Lockheed's Burbank, California, plant in a C-5A transport and assembled at Nellis AFB near Las Vegas. The prototype first flew in November 1977, near Groom Dry Lake at the Tonopah Test Range attached to Nellis AFB.

Nellis AFB was an ideal place to test the XST prototype because the U.S. Air Force's squadron of Soviet-built fighters—MiG-17, -19, -21, and -23 and Sukhoi Su-20 Fitters—is based at nearby Tonopah Base in Mud Dry Lake, Nevada. These fighters are sometimes referred to as the ''MiG Squadron,'' but the unit's official title is ''4477th *Test & Evaluation Squadron*'' (TES), and goes by the call name of ''Red Eagles.'' Real and simulated Soviet air-defense radars and SAMs are also situated on the Nellis ranges. During tests of Lockheed's XST prototype, the stealth aircraft was flown against the Soviet systems and was said to have ''worked superbly.'' The XST proved efficient against radar, acoustic, electronic, infrared, and optical detection systems.

In 1980, as testing of the XST prototypes showed promising results, the DOD lifted the curtain of secrecy surrounding the program at the Pentagon news conference (see Chapter 2). For the first time, it was admitted that stealth aircraft were being test-flown and that these aircraft "cannot be successfully intercepted with existing defense systems."

The XST was tested against many types of radar, including bistatic and low- and high-frequency types. Some of the radars were Soviet-built, while others were modified to simulate Soviet radars. In testing the detection and tracking capabilities of the radars against the XST, one source said that "It worked better than we had any right to expect, and it is exciting because it could cause the Soviets to spend billions of rubles to modify their entire existing air-defense forces, and even then they would get no guarantees, as the stealth technology continues to mature."

Crashes

More than one prototype XST was built, and two, perhaps three, were lost in crashes during testing. In the first two crashes, the aircraft's stealth characteristics were not accused of contributing to the accidents, but cost-cutting measures and accelerated construction of the aircraft were considered contributory factors. The first two crashes, in 1979 and the other in 1980, received little attention because they happened inside the boundaries of the Nellis Range.

The third reported crash of a stealth fighter occurred July 11, 1986, and gained considerable attention. This aircraft was thought to have been an operational version of Lockheed's XST prototype, called the F-19—which is now known to be designated F-117A—or perhaps a Northrop stealth aircraft designated TSA and was being flown by Air Force Maj. Ross Mulhare of the 4450th Tactical Air Group at Nellis AFB. Mulhare was killed when, it is believed, the stealth aircraft's engine failed and exploded, rupturing the main fuel tanks and causing the aircraft to explode and smash into a hillside.

The only reason the crash generated so much publicity was that it happened outside the secure Nellis Range, in a military operations area (MOA) called Complex 1A. The aircraft was being flown on a night training mission when it exploded and crashed into a hillside near the Kern River 14 miles northeast of Bakersfield, California, at about 2:00 A.M. A witness, who was flying a light aircraft a few miles from the crash site, reported that he saw the bright light from the explosion.

An Air Force officer publicly said that "the aircraft apparently exploded in midair while it was flying a low-level operational training mission." These missions are usually flown late at night and at low levels and high speeds. Each flight is planned well in advance, and pilots are instructed to identify their aircraft as either an A-7 Corsair II or some other operational tactical aircraft, to conceal the identity of their stealth fighters.

It took firefighters 16 hours to extinguish the fire from the crash. Local and federal officials and firefighters at the scene were told by Air Force investigators not to discuss what they had seen or heard at the crash site. The local firefighters were not allowed near the wreckage, which was cordoned off by the USAF. Authorities warned civilian pilots not to fly directly over the crash site.

Air Force officials investigating the crash said the aircraft "was not an F-19." If they had admitted it was an F-19 (it might have been Northrop's TSA), they would finally have confirmed the existence of the ultrasecret F-19 (F-117A). Another F-117A crashed on October 14, 1987, near Nellis AFB, killing Major Michael Stewart. No details of this crash are available.

The fourth reported crash of one of these stealth aircraft occurred November 16, 1987. An aircraft, described by Pentagon sources as a top-secret stealth fighter, crashed in a rugged desert area, killing the pilot. Major Victor Andrijauskas, a USAF official at Nellis AFB, Nevada, stated that the aircraft was flying over the Nellis gunnery range when it crashed. Another Pentagon official said at the time that the plane was similar to the one that crashed in California the year before (1986).

One retired Air Force general reportedly has stated the procedures of stealth fighter pilots that might run into trouble with their plane in flight: "Anyone who flies the Lockheed bird has orders that the article must never land anywhere but at its nest. If you can't bring it home, then you auger it in, preferably over water—even if you have to go in with it. The program cannot and will not be compromised. Period."

Lt. General Robert Bond was one of the leading figures close to the Lockheed/Air Force program and probably knew more about the XST test program than anyone else. Bond was killed in 1984, however, in the crash of a Soviet MiG-23 Flogger in the Tonopah Test Range. Bond had been vice commander of the Air Force Aeronautical Systems Command and was directly involved in the flight testing of the XST prototypes and the operational stealth fighters.

The F-117A

The XST prototypes successfully proved the stealth fighter concept, and in mid-1981 the government awarded Lockheed a contract to cover initial production of a full-size version of the XST—a reconnaissance/strike aircraft called the F-117A. The generic project name is SENIOR TREND. There are clues that indicate as much as $1 billion was included in the U.S. government's FY1983 budget to continue funding of the initial batch of 20 aircraft. A subsequent contract is believed to have been placed for at least 100 more of the F-117A fighters, since reduced to a total of 59.

The F-117A made its first flight in June 1981 from Tonopah Base, having been ferried, like its predecessors, from Lockheed's Skunkworks in a C-5A transport. F-117A production is believed to be taking place at Lockheed's Burbank facility, which might explain the occasional evening departures of C-5As from Burbank. The C-5As are presumably carrying unassembled F-117As or, it has been reported, F-117As with wings folded, to Tonopah or other final-assembly locations.

F-117A Appearance

During testing, XST prototypes could occasionally be seen from public roads near Tonopah, Nevada. According to witnesses who have seen the XST, the aircraft is "deltoid and batlike" in appearance. They also said it is highly maneuverable (contrary to some reports), with an estimated wingspan of 18 feet and a length of 35 feet. In profile, the XST is slender, and it has a tinted one-piece finely faired canopy covering the single-seat cockpit. The canopy used on the operational F-117A has flat radar-scattering panels and a V-shaped windshield.

The engines were modified nonafterburning General Electric CJ610 turbojets. Afterburning engines were not needed because the XST was not designed to fly at supersonic speeds. The forward fuselage and wing portion is made of angled flat surfaces that look like a wide inverted V-shape. The aircraft, viewed from any angle, is said to have a sort of rounded appearance.

Both the XST and F-117A reportedly have folding wings that would allow them to be shipped to bases in a C-5A transport. That is probably one reason why F-117As haven't made any long-range flights. F-117As also are said not to be capable of in-flight refueling because the refueling receptacle would be easily detectable by radar. A tanker aircraft dispatched to refuel a stealth fighter would only attract attention to the fighter, compromising the stealth fighter's capability of remaining undetected.

The F-117A fighter is illustrated in FIG. 7-1 and the color section. Many drawings, artists' impressions, and plastic model kits purport to reveal the real shape of the F-117A, but the true shape of the F-117A only became apparent when the Air Force released a grainy photograph of the aircraft late 1988.

Other drawings that have been published, followed by model kits, range from exotic-looking representations of the F-117A to downright ridiculous "conceptions." Most of these drawings are simply based on the artist's imagination, and even when artists are privy to some of the classified details of the F-117A, they seem to ignore such information when creating conceptions. The F-117A model kit produced by Testor Corp. does not resemble the real F-117A; the kit looks more like Lockheed's unmanned Mach 4 D-21B drone.

The Air Force photo of the F-117A shown in this book is an exception. The following details, culled from various sources, are the most accurate on the F-117A ever published.

Fig. 7-1. The F-117A Nighthawk.(Courtesy U.S. Air Force)

◇ The aircraft's *official* designation, is F-117A.
◇ It has rounded surfaces (airframe).
◇ Its shape is similar to that of NASA's space shuttle.
◇ The F-117A resembles some of the lifting-body research aircraft tested by NASA and the U.S. Air Force (and made famous by the opening scene in the TV series "Six Million Dollar Man".
◇ Dorsal engine air intakes are fitted conformally with the upper portion of the fuselage and wing structure.
◇ Twin vertical fins are canted outward, not inward.
◇ There are single- and two-seat (tandem) versions.
◇ The aircraft is about the same size and weight as an F/A-18 Hornet or F-4 Phantom II.
◇ The landing gear is not stalky or squat, but appears more like that of an F-15.

A comparison of these features with the drawings of the F-117A, and XST prototype, and photograph of the F-117A shows that the features match the drawings very closely.

Did Benson Help Design the F-117A?

Anyone familiar with the work of Cmdr. William Benson of Aero-Marine Research might notice that the F-117A resembles Benson's XD-110B RPV. In 1976, Benson demonstrated his RPV to the U.S. Air Force and military officials from Israel and Japan. According to an edition of the authoritative *Jane's All the World's Aircraft*. "The RPV versions of the XD-110 Series had attracted considerable interest from the aerospace industry and from military services in the U.S. as well as from overseas. Several of these RPVs were involved in research programs, and the advanced technology derived from these deltas has been incorporated into several designs produced for or by other companies."

That was the last the media wrote about Benson and his RPVs. Coincidentally, 1976 was the same year DARPA and the Air Force chose Lockheed to build the XST prototype for the HAVE BLUE program. Benson reportedly was asked to join Clarence "Kelly" Johnson at Lockheed's Skunkworks as a consultant, and it has been said that the F-117A design is based directly on the design of Benson's patented pure-wing delta used on his RPVs. (Pure-wing refers to the fact that the wing chord is the same dimension as the fuselage length.)

Features of Benson's XD-110 Series that might have found their way into the F-117A design include: stall-proof, with full controllability at low airspeeds in a mushing condition; excellent STOL (short-takeoff and landing) capability; and almost nonexistent radar, infrared, and visual signatures.

Benson planned to build a full-scale aircraft based on the XD-110 design, to be called the "Benson 110 Nova" and feature a two-seat tandem cockpit. In 1976, Benson said that a prototype of the 110 Nova was under construction, but that was the last heard publicly of the project. Perhaps Lockheed built the 110 Nova as the XST prototypes.

One of the major reasons Lockheed was chosen to build the F-117A is that it had the most experience building manned stealth aircraft. Because the U.S. Air Force was looking for a stealth aircraft for covert missions and knew of Benson's plans for the full-scale 110 Nova, it is possible the Air Force decided to blend Lockheed's stealth experience with the inherent low-observable features of Benson's pure-wing delta design.

F-117A Construction

The primary RAM and infrared-reflecting material used on the F-117A is Dow Chemical's Fibaloy (see Chapter 5). Fibaloy is used for structural airframe parts in the F-117A and for skin panels, spars, ribs, and longerons. Only 10 percent of the airframe's structural weight is from metal. Reinforced carbon fiber, developed by the Air Force Materials Laboratory at Wright Patterson AFB in Dayton, Ohio, is another important RAM used on the F-117A. This material not only absorbs radar energy, but dissipates it as well and helps reduce the F-117A's infrared signature. It is used primarily for high-temperature areas like outer skin panels near the engines, and wing and vertical-fin leading edges.

The F-117A's unique shape is one factor that contributes to RCS reduction. Edges are rounded, and skins are made of Fibaloy in a secret and difficult manufacturing process. These skins are built in multiple layers that are filled with bubbles and tiny fibers oriented in a specific alignment, spacing, and density for maximum RCS reduction. This process is probably the most secret element of stealth technology. Parts are formed using super-plastics (see Chapter 5) and are joined with strong adhesives.

Internal structural architecture of the F-117A probably has an even greater effect on RCS reduction. A design called *cut-diamond*, which employs several thousand flat surfaces, reportedly is used on the F-117A. Each of the small, flat surfaces is angled so it does not share a common radar reflective angle with any other small, flat surface. When a radar beam strikes the F-117A, only one or two of the flat surfaces reflects the incoming radar energy, while the adjacent surfaces present too high an incident angle to reflect the radar energy back to the radar receiver.

The cut-diamond structure is covered by a layer of Fibaloy that is said to be able to absorb 98 percent of all radiated energy. Like the SR-71, internal plastic radar-absorbing triangular inserts are fitted to the F-117A's vertical-fin and wing leading edges. Iron ball RAM is applied to external surfaces and to some internal metal parts. All gear doors and access panels are specially shaped and tightly fitted to maintain the airframe's low RCS.

To enhance its low visual signature, the F-117A might employ active and passive background-masking camouflage techniques that enable it to change color to match the background. It is reported that two camouflage colors are used: flat-black for night missions, and dull gray for day missions.

A more likely active camouflage technique is referred to by a retired Air Force officer as "background-clutter signal to aircraft RCS matching." This technique makes use of the F-117's extensive ECM/ESM suite and does not require any changes to the aircraft's structure. With this technique, an F-117A flying at low level can protect itself from look-down interceptor radars by matching its overall RCS (as detected from above) with that of the terrain below. This ability would make the F-117A show up as ground clutter on the interceptor's radar, provided the F-117A's RCS precisely matches that of the terrain below it, and the hostile radars would simply reject the clutter and the F-117A masked in the clutter, and never detect the F-117A.

ECM/ESM equipment is housed in *smart skins*, or portions of the F-117A's airframe that incorporate microcircuitry, thus avoiding the need to install antennae or sensors that might have a high RCS on the outside of the airframe. This feature has the combined benefit of saving space on the inside of the airframe and permitting the airframe to be lighter and smaller.

Reconnaissance/weapons systems include a forward-looking laser radar used for both terrain-following navigation and for attacking targets. A forward-looking infrared (FLIR) system is installed, as well as a low light level TV and a head-up display. Its weapons suite reportedly includes the optically guided AGM-65 missile and the AGM-45 Shrike antiradiation missile. (Antiradiation missiles detect and attack hostile radar sites that actively emit radar energy.) The AGM-88A high-speed antiradiation missile (HARM) also might be included. An advanced gun system developed by Hughes called the *in-weather survivable gun system/covert* is installed, and all weapons are carried internally.

Another weapon that might be used is the AGM-136A Tacit Rainbow antiradiation drone missile (see Chapter 10). This weapon can loiter after release and protect the F-117A from hostile radar tracking by detecting and destroying hostile radars. The Tacit Rainbow is small enough that four can be carried internally by the F-117A.

In one reported test of the F-117A's weapon aiming and guidance system, a 500-lb bomb was dropped from altitude of 10,000 feet, and the bomb scored, going right into the top of its target, a 55-gallon drum.

Lear Siegler developed a guadruple redundant electronic fly-by-wire system for the F-117A that eliminates the need for control cables, thus saving weight and simplifying construction. The pilot controls the F-117A with a side-stick controller mounted on the right side of the cockpit.

The F-117A pilot sits on an ACES ejection seat. The pilot's canopy has flat surfaces, and should be coated with an optically transparent RAM to prevent radar reflection from the pilot or cockpit equipment. Landing gear is designed for rough-field operations, and each gear leg has a single wheel.

Infrared signature is reduced by mixing fan-bypass air and air from cooling baffles with exhaust gases. Mixing of air with exhaust also has the benefit of reducing the acoustic signature. Because infrared homing missiles track aircraft by the heat of their exhaust nozzles, not the heat of the exhaust gas, the nozzles are made of materials that keep the infrared signature low. Cooling baffles and special coatings also help reduce the infrared signature from hot engine-exhaust nozzles. Newer infrared homing missiles with all-aspect launch angles can track only the exhaust plume, but the work done to cool exhaust nozzles and cool exhaust gases on the F-117A and other stealth aircraft makes infrared lock-on by these kinds of missiles highly unlikely.

Two modified nonafterburning 12,500-lb General Electric F404-HB turbofan engines are said to power the F-117A. Two-dimensional thrust-vectoring exhaust nozzles, which can vector thrust in various vertical and horizontal positions, are reportedly installed; however, it is likely the nozzles are only two-dimensional in shape, with no vectoring capability.

Material around the engine bays is a matrix sandwich of polymers and pyramidic noise-absorbing structures. The sound-proofing is so effective that the F-117A is said to make a medium-level humming noise at a distance of 100 feet, and on takeoff a slight whine is heard. The F-117A might use a Benson-designed Rotorduct system that provides additional cold thrust from the engines. If installed, the Rotorduct system is probably connected to the forward and aft sections of the engines.

During night operations, the F-117A flies lights out, with no navigation, strobe, or position lights of any kind. F-117As are equipped for all-weather operations without any outside assistance. All guidance systems are passive, except for the laser-radar, but that gives no signals that could be detected. Guidance systems might include a ring-laser gyrobased inertial navigation system and global positioning system receiver, both of which are passive navigation systems.

Although the F-117A can fly at supersonic speeds, most of its flying is done below the speed of sound close to the ground to take advantage of terrain-masking of hostile radar installations. High-speed flight at low levels also protects the F-117A from infrared-guided weapons or infrared detection systems. At higher altitudes, the F-117A would be exposed to such systems for longer periods of time, while at low levels, the F-117A is not over one area long enough for weapons systems to lock on. Even if the weapons could lock on briefly, the F-117A flies so quickly that it would be long gone before the weapon could shoot it down.

Operating at high speeds and low levels makes the F-117A somewhat unstable due to its large wing/fuselage planform. This might be one reason, among others, for one or two of the known crashes. It has not yet been confirmed, but the F-117A might use small ride-control vanes similar to those on the nose of the B-1 bomber. These are known as *impedance-loaded flow-control vanes*, and they alleviate the often bumpy ride encountered during low-level and high-speed flight.

Supersonic flight in the F-117A might be inefficient because of the materials from which it is built. Some of the materials, while excellent at reducing detectability signatures, have a rough finish that could add to the F-117A's parasite drag.

An F-117A unit is permanently based at Tonopah Base (Area 30, also known as Sandia Strip and Mellon Strip) in the northwest corner of the highly secret Nellis Test Range about 170 miles from Las Vegas, in Nevada. Tonopah Base has 72 hangars and was refurbished in 1979-80 by the U.S. Air Force. (It hadn't been used since World War II.) The Air Force will admit to the base's existence, but won't comment on the aircraft stationed there. The unit is known as *Team One—Furtim Vigilans* (covert vigilantes), and there are between 75 and 100 F-117As based there. (The term literally means "vigilant by stealth" or "stealthily vigilant" in Latin.) The full-service F-117A wing gained initial operational capability in 1983 at Tonopah Base.

There are F-117A temporary-duty (TDY) detachments at Elmendorf AFB and Shemya AFB in Alaska, Kadena Air Base in Japan, and in the United Kingdom. The F-117A also reportedly has been active in the Middle East and in Latin America.

The U.S. Air Force uses the F-117A in various roles and has integrated F-117A operations with those of the rapid-deployment forces and with the new special operations command. Two of the F-117A's known missions are covert reconnaissance and covert surgical strikes on preselected targets. In operational tests, this effective stealth aircraft has reportedly flown within 20 miles of actual Soviet-manned radar stations without being detected.

F-117A Nighthawk Specifications

Length	About 56 ft
Height	About 16 ft
Wingspan	About 40 ft
Empty weight	About 20,000 lb
Maximum takeoff weight	About 34,000 lb
Cruise speed	Mach 0.8 to 0.9
Maximum speed	Mach 1.0 at 36,000 ft
Powerplant	Two 12,500 lb GE F404-HB nonafterburning turbofans highly modified. Composites used in engine construction
Combat radius	400 miles

F-19/RF-19 Stealth Fighter

Some sources indicate that the F-19/RF-19 stealth aircraft does exist; that is, it is not the same aircraft as the F-117A. Some facts about the F-19 revealed by sources involved with the program include the following:

◇ The F-19 is a pure stealth design and is within the U.S. DOD's black programs.
◇ It was (and may be operational now) part of the original HAVE BLUE XST stealth prototyping program, with demonstrators flying in 1977. (The F-117A is part of the SENIOR TREND program.)
◇ Its detail design is different from the F-117A Nighthawk's.
◇ It is thought to carry out reconnaissance and is capable of supersonic flight.
◇ Its basic planform is similar to that of the U.S. space shuttle.
◇ It is a single-seat, single-engine aircraft.

LOCKHEED/AIR FORCE AURORA HYPERSONIC STEALTH RECONNAISSANCE AIRCRAFT

This program, code-named AURORA, has been confirmed by a retired Air Force official, who said, "USAF has had this type of aircraft on the drawing board for many years now." The name *Aurora* was thought to have belonged to the B-2 bomber or F-117 stealth fighter, but it is now known to refer to a super-secret hypersonic long-range stealth aircraft designed and built at Lockheed's Skunkworks in Burbank, California (FIG. 7-2). There have been reports of Auroras flying from Nellis AFB's Area 51 (Watertown Strip) in Groom Dry Lake, Nevada.

Fig. 7-2. An artist's concept of a hypervelocity vehicle, which was discussed during NATO meetings in September 1986. (U.S. Air Force art, courtesy U.S. Department of Defense)

The Aurora's top speed is said to be 3,800 miles per hour or more and cruise range 5,750 miles. Operational altitude is between 100,000 and 150,000 feet. With those performance figures, it is likely that the Aurora is intended to replace the aging fleet of Lockheed SR-71 strategic reconnaissance aircraft.

The disclosure of the Aurora Mach 5 stealth spy aircraft was apparently made by mistake by the DOD in its 1985 defense budget proposal. One budget document, with the title "Air Breathing Reconnaissance," contained a passing reference to the Lockheed SR-71 spy plane. This was followed by lines that referred to the SR-71's replacement, with the program code name of AURORA.

According to reports from various aviation authorities, since 1980, Lockheed and the USAF have been testing a Mach 6 hypersonic research, air-breathing, manned aircraft from the secret test range on Area 51 (Groom Lake, Nevada). These reports also state that the Aurora aircraft stemmed from that research program.

During mid-1987 congressional hearings, information about AURORA was nearly leaked, but only scant details of the program are known to the public. The Air Force has begun reducing the operational number of SR-71s in inventory during the past few years, so observers of stealth aircraft knew something was up. Air Force Secretary Edward Aldridge explained that SR-71 retirements were simply a result of the expense of operating the Blackbird, but he also admitted that the Air Force is interested in developing a manned reconnaissance aircraft incorporating low-observable technology. The Aurora could be the aircraft sought by the Air Force as an SR-71 replacement.

The Mach 5.8 Aurora's engines run on liquid methane. After taking off from Watertown Strip and refueling once in flight, the Aurora reportedly can cross the Pacific Ocean nonstop in 2.5 hours. A modified KC-10 or KC-135 tanker aircraft is said to be used for inflight refueling of the Aurora.

The AURORA program was allocated $2.3 billion in 1985. One report stated that there are 25 of the secret hypersonic spy planes already operational from Tonapah Base Area 30 in Nevada.

Two or three personnel, seated in tandem, operate the Aurora. Its external shape is said to be of double-delta design, with conformal wing and fuselage blending. The Aurora's RCS is probably low, near that of the F-117A, which is from 0.1 to .203 square meter.

According to another retired DOD official, "With the SR-71 Blackbird, they [the Soviets] know we're there, but they can't touch us. With the Aurora, they won't even know we're there."

Lockheed has been studying hypersonic aircraft that fly from Mach 4 to Mach 7 and up to 250,000 feet for years, so it comes as no surprise that an aircraft like the Aurora is flying.

NORTHROP/BOEING B-2
ADVANCED TECHNOLOGY BOMBER (ATB)

In April 1988, the U.S. Air Force released an artist's concept of the B-2 ATB showing the basic shape of the stealth bomber (see FIG. 7-3 and color section). An actual photograph of the B-2 was revealed later in 1988, and the B-2 was shown for the first time at a rollout ceremony November 22, 1988, at Northrop's Palmdale, California, facility. Because the Air Force allowed the public to view the B-2, it is unlikely that the artist's conception and photo it released was intended to be a form of disinformation for the Soviets.

B-2 Background

The decision to proceed with the B-2 stems from a conclusion in 1980 by then President Jimmy Carter and Defense Secretary Harold Brown that the B-1 bomber would be unable to penetrate Soviet defenses successfully beyond 1990. After the B-1 program was derailed, the Carter Administration decided that positive results

Fig. 7-3. The B-2 bomber. (Courtesy U.S. Air Force)

of the HAVE BLUE studies were justification for launch of a full-scale low-observable penetrating bomber program.

Two contractor teams responded to the request for proposals for an ATB: Lockheed/Rockwell and Northrop/Boeing. These companies had already completed studies of advanced bombers that included many possible aircraft configurations—from scissor-wing designs to pure delta-wing planforms. The Lockheed/Rockwell team chose to offer a high-altitude supersonic penetrating bomber based on Lockheed's F-19A stealth fighter, but scaled up to bomber size. Northrop/Boeing designed a subsonic flying-wing type aircraft that could operate at both high and low altitudes.

No doubt Northrop was taking advantage of its extensive experience with flying-wing designs. It is ironic to note that while Northrop's post-World War II YB-49 flying-wing bomber was ordered in large quantities by the U.S. government, then suddenly canceled for reasons that have never been explained, Northrop now appears to be vindicating its founder's early affinity for flying-wing designs. One factor that might be important for a stealth bomber is that a flying wing is difficult to see when viewed in profile.

Boeing also had done some research in the early 1970s on low-observable aircraft. Thus, the company was well equipped to team up with Northrop on the B-2 program.

The Air Force chose the Northrop/Boeing proposal for further development and issued contracts for detailed design and construction of one or more prototype preproduction aircraft, to be designated *YB-2*. The design of the basic B-2 shape was first flight-tested in 1982 as three subscale proof-of-concept demonstrator prototypes from Groom Lake, Nevada. The Air Force plans to order 132 B-2s, provided flight testing this year is successful, at a cost of $36.6 billion in 1981 dollars. That figure was later revised upward to $43 billion because of increased program costs, then it was upped another 20 percent by the Air Force. In 1989 dollars, adjusted for inflation since 1981, the total cost is now estimated to be some $520 million per bomber, or a mind-boggling $68.6 billion for the entire program—further evidence that stealth technology does not come cheap.

B-1 VERSUS B-2

The B-1B bomber depends on low-level penetration of hostile radar defenses to complete its mission. It is not able to detect or track mobile targets because of its low altitude, unless it pops above the horizon momentarily. Doing so would make it vulnerable to enemy detection, however, so the B-1B is effectively limited to remaining at low altitudes and avoiding mobile targets that it can't engage. The B-2 bomber, with its stealth capabilities, will be able to operate at higher altitudes without being detected, thus enabling it to detect, track, and engage important mobile targets. The B-2's stealth technology is an order of magnitude more sophisticated than that used in the B-1B.

A full-scale engineering mockup of the B-2 was completed in late 1985 at Northrop's Pico Rivera, California, Advanced Systems Division. Construction of the B-2 is underway at the Pico Rivera facility, which Northrop renamed the "B-2 Division" on May 18, 1988, because most work at that facility is connected with the B-2 program. Boeing shares overall responsibility for the program with Northrop, and LTV and General Electric are major subcontractors. Four 19,000-lb GE-F118-GE-100 turbofan engines power the B-2.

The B-2 was originally intended to be roughly the same size as the Soviet Tupolev Tu-26 Backfire bomber, with a maximum takeoff weight of about 280,000 pounds. The final design of the B-2 is much larger, however, and it now compares with the B-1B in size and weight. Maximum takeoff weight is about 400,000 pounds, and payload, 40,000 pounds. The B-2 will be able to fly up to Mach 0.85 and will have a 5,750-mile unrefueled range.

According to the Air Force drawing, the B-2 is triangular in shape, with a bulbous cockpit blended smoothly into the center of the wing and flanked by two blended engine pods containing two engines each. Cockpit windows are load-bearing parts of the airframe structure and blend smoothly with the raised-hump cockpit and the nose of the aircraft. *Aviation Week & Space Technology* magazine speculates that the trailing edge's saw-tooth design might be intended to mask the engines' infrared signature. There was some initial concern at Northrop about stability because of the lack of vertical fins, but with computer-controlled flight controls, that should not be a problem.

The B-2's RCS is said to be about one-millionth of a square meter, which makes its radar response similar to that of a hummingbird. Contributing to the low RCS is the B-2's internal structure, much of which is titanium coated with epoxy graphite composites. Computer-aided design techniques were used to obtain what is known as *sensor-defeating architecture* and the inherent low-observable shape of the B-2. A new aluminum-lithium alloy (7050), about 10 percent lighter than conventional alloys used in aircraft construction, is used in the B-2.

A type of anechoic filtering structure is found throughout the B-2. This structure involves combinations of plastics, epoxy graphite, carbon fibers, and ceramics worked into loose molecular structures filled with irregular, porous, radar energy-baffling honeycombs. Like sound-absorbing structures in anechoic chambers, these materials capture radar or infrared energy and bounce it around inside the honeycomb until the energy is either absorbed or dissipated.

To reduce the engine's potential of reflecting radar energy, many major engine installation components are made of RAM. Snakelike air-intake ducts have carbon-composite baffles to keep radar energy away from the compressor face. Dense carbon-grain packing in the composite materials around the engine bay absorb radar energy entering the fan sections of the engines and dissipate midengine heat. Ultradense carbon foams absorb and cool engine heat, reducing its infrared signature. Active and passive infrared countermeasures (IRCMs) are also used, as well as ferrite-based RAM like iron ball.

The B-2 will be pushing the technology envelope in a number of new areas. Flight controls are fly-by-light using fiberoptics, and fly-by-wire. Fly-by-light control systems have an important advantage over electric wire: the fiberoptics don't conduct electromagnetic pulse generated by nuclear explosions and thus do not need to be shielded against EMP. Some control systems will use voice-activation, where the pilot will simply tell the system what to do instead of pushing a button, and artificial intelligence will be incorporated into much of the B-2's computerized systems. Other features include: phased forward-looking laser radar and millimeter radar for detecting and tracking mobile targets; FLIR and low-light level TV sensors; and terrain-profile matching, ring-laser gyro inertial nav, and global positioning system for passive navigation guidance.

General Dynamics' AGM-129A air-launched cruise missile and Boeing's AGM-131A SRAM II will be carried in a standard rotary launcher in the B-2's internal weapons bays. The AGM-136A Tacit Rainbow antiradiation drone missile likely will be carried when it becomes available. Other weapons under consideration are an airborne self-defense laser, electromagnetic rail guns, and conventional bombs with nonnuclear warheads.

Two types of explosives could be used for the warheads. Spin-polarized hydrogen has one-hundred times the energy of nitroglycerin but needs absolute zero temperatures to operate. Metastable-helium has the same explosive power but is more easily formed into solids than can be triggered.

The first flight of the prototype B-2 was scheduled for early 1989 to Edwards AFB from the final assembly facility at the Air Force's Plant 42 in Palmdale, California. The prototype is about one year behind schedule as a result of technical problems with the aircraft's construction, including wiring problems, cracks in composite wing leading edges, incompatibility between engines and air intakes, and stress discontinuities in the load-bearing windshield. IOC is not anticipated until the mid-1990s, and the first deployment base is expected to be Whiteman AFB in Missouri.

During the wait for the B-2's first flight, B-2 avionics and flight-control systems tests have been underway in a flight-test vehicle flying from Edwards AFB.

B-2 ATB Specifications

Length	69 ft
Wingspan	172 ft
Height	17 ft
Lowest fuselage ground clearance	7 to 8 ft
Maximum takeoff weight	400,000 lb
Payload	40,000 lb (Note: Only 120 out of the planned 132 total B-2s will be assigned the nuclear-strike penetration role. They will have a combined weapon load of 2,000 warheads.)
Range, unrefueled	6,000 + nautical miles; capable of in-flight refueling.
Speed	Mach 0.85
Rollout & first flight	B-2 "Ship-One," mid-November 1988 and early 1989, respectively. Second B-2 construction is well underway. First six B-2s will undergo testing at Edwards AFB, five of which will enter service.
Accommodation	Two-man crew

Contractors working on B-2 program:

Prime Contractor: Northrop Corp.
Major Subcontractors:

1. Boeing Advanced Systems Division (airframe components)
2. Boeing Military Airplane Company (will produce the B-2's Advanced Applications Rotary Weapons Launcher. This will not necessarily be a derivative of Boeing's Common Strategic Rotary Launcher as fitted to the B-52H and B-1B bombers, but will utilize current technology.)
3. General Electric Aircraft Engines Group (F118 engines)
4. Honeywell Corp. (avionics)
5. Hughes Aircraft Radar Systems Group (radar and avionics)
6. LTV Aircraft Products Group (airframe components)
7. Link Flight Simulation Corp. (B-2 training simulators)

NORTHROP TACTICAL STEALTH AIRCRAFT

Northrop is reported to have signed contracts with the U.S. Air Force in 1982 to build up to 100 tactical stealth aircraft (TSA). The TSA, about which little is known, is said to have been the type that crashed north of Bakersfield in July 1986. At least 20 American black programs are now in progress, so it is difficult to say which stealth aircraft might have been involved in that crash. Most industry personnel believe it was a Lockheed F-19, but others say it was the TSA, which is similar to a design Lockheed proposed to the Air Force in the late 1970s, that crashed.

If it wasn't an F-19 or TSA, the crashed stealth aircraft could have been one of three subscale proof-of-concept flying wing demonstrators that were used early in the B-2 program. These subscale aircraft are still being flown from secret airstrips in the Nellis Range in Nevada.

MCDONNELL DOUGLAS/GENERAL DYNAMICS A-12 ADVANCED TACTICAL AIRCRAFT

The McDonnell Douglas/General Dynamics team won this important U.S. Navy contract to build a stealth replacement for the aging A-6 Intruder day/night, all-weather naval attack bomber (FIG. 2-4). The Northrop/Grumman team lost the competition.

Plans for a replacement for the A-6 have been underway since the mid-1970s, when the Navy commissioned a feasibility study for an A-6 replacement known as VAMX. The advanced tactical aircraft (ATA) was officially approved by the Navy and the DOD in the early 1980s as an aircraft to be developed under American black programs.

Fig. 7-4. Grumman's A-6F Intruder II modified attack aircraft was developed by the Navy as an interim attack aircraft and will fulfill that role until the Navy's new A-12 advanced tactical aircraft (ATA) comes on line with combat units in the late 1990s. The A-12 ATA will replace all A-6 Intruders in service with the Navy and Marines. (Courtesy U.S. Navy)

The first flight of the ATA, designated ''A-12,'' is expected in 1990 or 1991. According to a source close to the program, the A-12 ''is a stealthy A-6.'' (see FIG. 7-5.) It seats two crewmembers and will fly at subsonic speeds. It is powered by two General Electric F404 turbofan engines with two-dimensional exhaust nozzles. Maximum takeoff weight will be in the 50,000- to 55,000-pound weight class, and the weapons payload will be 12,000 pounds, carried either in conformal external housings or internally. Mission-adaptive wings (MAWs) that can vary their camber depending on the flight profile probably will be incorporated in the A-12 design.

The A-12's primary weapon might be the proposed Navy advanced interdiction weapon system (AIWS), which is a standoff weapon intended to replace several conventional weapons now in inventory. Standard tactical aircraft weapons will fit

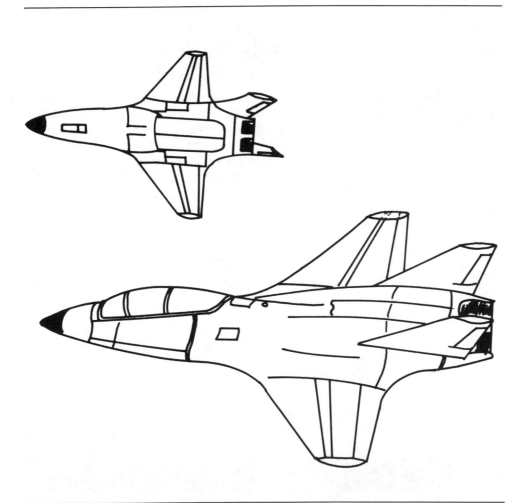

Fig. 7-5. Illustration of a possible configuration for an advanced tactical aircraft (ATA) to fulfill a Navy requirement for an aircraft to replace the A-6 Intruder. The Air Force might consider the ATA as a replacement for its F-111 and F-15E interdictors.

on the A-12, and self-defense weapons could include the AIM-120 AMRAAM active-radar guided missile, the infrared-guided AIM-132 ASRAAM, and the advanced air-to-air missile (AAAM) under development. It is not known if the ATA will have an internal gun.

A new all-weather, multipurpose radar is being developed for the A-12 and will be used for air-to-ground and air-to-air modes, as well as for some passive techniques. A laser radar might be part of the A-12's advanced sensor system. Other avionics will include the integrated electronic warfare system (INEWS) and the integrated communication, navigation, and identification avionics (ICNIA) system, both of which will be 90 percent compatible with avionics systems slated for the Air Force's advanced tactical fighter (ATF).

The Navy has said it wants to acquire at least 450 A-12s, which will cost from $93 million to $100 million each. Another 550 might be manufactured if the Air Force decides to replace its F-111 and F-15E with the A-12 by the year 2000. According to a knowledgeable source, contractors that competed for the ATA program said range and speed of the A-12 is lower than the original specifications set by the Navy because the requirements could not be met for the price the Navy was willing to pay for the aircraft.

The McDonnell Douglas/General Dynamics A-12 ATA contractor team selected subcontractors on the program in April 1988. The subcontractors and their responsibilities are as follows:

◇ Allied Signal Aerospace Co.'s Garrett Control—conventional air data computer system.
◇ General Electric's Aircraft Electronics Division—missile warning system.
◇ Harris Corporations Government Aerospace Systems Division—multifunction antenna system.
◇ Litton Aero Products' Amecom Division—electronics surveillance measures set.
◇ Texas Instruments and United's Norden Systems Division—multifunction radar system.
◇ Westinghouse Electric Corp.—combined function forward-looking infrared (FLIR) system.

GENERAL DYNAMICS MODEL 100

General Dynamics is developing or possibly already testing a stealth aircraft called the Model 100. It is not known whether it is manned or unmanned, or even what mission the aircraft is to fulfill or what branch of the military is funding the aircraft. General Dynamics engineers involved with the Model 100 project are under strict internal orders not to speak, even to other General Dynamics engineers, about the Model 100.

AIR FORCE ADVANCED TACTICAL FIGHTER— LOCKHEED YF-22 AND NORTHROP YF-23

The advanced tactical fighter breaks hard right; it just entered hostile airspace. The pilot lies nearly prone in his articulating ejection seat, his arms forced tightly to his sides by the G-forces. All vital situation information is projected on his helmet-mounted display system, and his eyes scan the symbols on the display for targets. When he spots a target, aided by the ATF's sophisticated sensor systems, he need only look at the control for whatever weapons system he wishes to engage and speak a command to fire the weapon.

The display lights up: a hostile aircraft has just entered sensor range. The G-forces build again as the pilot maneuvers to get in position for a shot at the enemy, a Soviet Su-27 Flanker whose pilot doesn't know that he has blundered into range of the ATF's sensors or that the ATF's pilot can engage the Flanker without visually identifying his target and well before the Flanker pilot realizes he is in trouble. The pilot allows the Flanker to get closer then, with a barked command into his facemask microphone, the pilot launches an AIM-132 ASRAAM at the Flanker. In a burst of orange flame, the missile scores a direct hit and the Flanker explodes. Target destroyed; the pilot relaxes slightly, but continues to monitor his helmet display as he speeds back to friendly territory at Mach 1.5.

This situation is hypothetical, but if the Air Force has its way, the aircraft described will become a reality. The program is, of course, classified, and calls for a twin-engine advanced tactical fighter (ATF) that will likely represent the next generation of fighter aircraft.

Design studies for the ATF have been underway since the early 1980s by seven aerospace companies, each of which submitted concepts to the U.S. Air Force. After the Air Force issued a formal request for proposals, some of the companies decided that the risks of the ATF program were too great for one company to take alone and so joined forces. In late 1986, two contractor teams and two individual companies responded to the ATF request for proposals. One team consisted of Lockheed, Boeing, and General Dynamics; the other team's members were Northrop and McDonnell Douglas. Grumman and Rockwell decided to compete for the contract on their own. Each member of each team and Grumman and Rockwell submitted their ATF designs (FIGS. 7-6 through 7-8) and the two winning proposals were Lockheed's and Northrop's. The other members of those two companies' teams became subcontractors to the winning companies.

In November 1986, the Air Force awarded $691 million contracts to each team to pay for construction of two prototype ATFs by each team. The aircraft will be subjected to a competitive fly-off to determine which company will win the contract. The first flight of an ATF prototype is scheduled for late 1989. Lockheed's work is centered at its Skunkworks (FIG. 7-9), and Northrop probably has its program set up at its Pico Rivera, California, plant (FIG. 7-10). The Northrop ATF designation is ''YF-23A'' and Lockheed's ATF designation is ''YF-22A.''

The Air Force wants to buy at least 750 ATFs by the year 2006, with annual production averaging 72 aircraft per year. Flyaway cost of each ATF is estimated at $35 million, which brings the total value of the contract to about $27 billion. The Navy might be interested in ATFs as well, and could order 400 to 600 ATF fighters to replace its F-14D fighters by the year 2000 (FIG. 7-11). More ATFs might be ordered by the Marines.

If the Navy chooses not to purchase the ATF, Grumman is prepared to propose what it calls the ''Tomcat-21'' version of the F-14. The Tomcat-21 involves advance

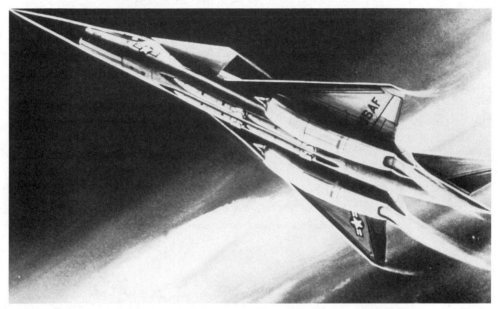

Fig. 7-6. A Boeing artist's concept of an advanced tactical aircraft-type fighter. (Courtesy U.S. Air Force)

Fig. 7-7. General Dynamics suggests another concept of an advanced tactical fighter in this painting. (Courtesy U.S. Air Force)

Fig. 7-8. Artist's concept of a proposed Rockwell International advanced tactical fighter-type aircraft. (Courtesy U.S. Air Force).

Fig. 7-9. This concept of a Lockheed advanced tactical fighter production line depicts manufacturing advances developed at Lockheed. Extensive use of robotics, paperless processes, and interchangeable tooling, completely integrated by computer, will increase quality and reduce production costs. Such a factory also will allow greater flexibility to absorb production surges. Lockheed planners believe these developments, combined with the introduction of new composite materials, will permit production of a fighter of unprecedented quality and durability. (Courtesy Lockheed-California Co.)

Fig. 7-10. *Northrop advanced tactical fighter concept.* (Courtesy U.S. Air Force)

Fig. 7-11. *Grumman/Navy F-14A-Plus, which might be replaced by the advanced tactical fighter if the Navy decides to purchase the ATF. So far, the Navy is monitoring the Air Force ATF program to see if the ATF will be useful as ship-based fighter.* (Courtesy U.S.Navy)

design techniques to reduce the radar cross section and infrared signature, new composite materials, and the addition of a ground attack capability to the F-14 design. Also being looked at are advanced technology engines, which might even be similar to those on the ATF.

Other proposals now include, the McDonnell Douglas "Hornet 2000," and an advanced and completely new design.

Lockheed YF-22 Features

Note: These features also apply to Northrop's YF-23.

◇ RCS considerably less than 10 percent that of the F-15.
◇ Capable of routine part-throttle nonafterburning supersonic cruise from 20,000 to 30,000 feet.
◇ Turn rate and thrust-to-weight ratio markedly superior to F-15, with excellent low-speed controllability.
◇ High reliability and maintainability, able to operate with less ground-support equipment than the F-15.
◇ Use of composites and new aluminum alloys for a 20 percent weight reduction compared to conventional all-metal airframes.
◇ Avionics five to ten times the capability of those in the F-15, with improved sensors, data processing, and cockpit tactical data automation.
◇ Takeoff weight reduction of 20 percent from improvements in technology over the last 20 years.

The expected shape of the YF-22, contrary to artists' conceptions that have already appeared, will be a delta-winged airframe with close-coupled canards forward of the wings and twin, outward-canted vertical fins. The wing will be an MAW featuring variable camber, and engine air intakes will be semiconformal. Stealth technology will be used to reduce all detectability signatures on the ATF, and it will also use advanced ECM technology.

Although Lockheed's design won the contest among that company's team members, each team member will contribute its expertise in building the YF-22. Lockheed is responsible for the forward fuselage, cockpit, and stealth technology to be used on the airframe, and will remain overall systems contractor to the Air Force. Boeing will build the wings and rear fuselage.

A Boeing MAW, with variable camber on both leading and trailing edges as opposed to conventional flaps and slats, is being tested on an F-111/AFTI jet, so Boeing's expertise with MAWs should be beneficial for the YF-22. Data from the F-111/AFTI program is being made available to the Northrop/McDonnell Douglas team as well. Boeing also has experience with thermoplastic construction techniques and has built a full-scale, high-temperature thermoplastic wing and a rear fuselage, incorporating graphite fibers to demonstrate advanced materials for use on the YF-22.

Boeing is responsible for producing the offensive avionics and mission software for the YF-22 and has selected a team consisting of General Electric and Martin Marietta to design the electro-optical infrared sensor system (EOSS) for the YF-22. EOSS will enable ATF pilots to penetrate hostile airspace, evade air defense radars, and conduct air-to-air combat missions against the newest Soviet aircraft, including the MiG-29 and Su-27.

General Dynamics is responsible for defensive avionics and communciation and navigation components. General Dynamics also has responsibility for the mid-fuselage, aircraft control surfaces, flight controls, and environmental, electrical, and hydraulic systems for the YF-22 ATF.

Lockheed will design the avionics architecture, cockpit controls and displays, and an expert system to help ATF pilots with effective, timely situation assessment and facilitate beyond-visual-range target identification. The system is called the electronic copilot (ECOP) by Lockheed, although the generic term *pilot's associate* is sometimes used.

Lockheed awarded a contract to Hughes Radar Systems Group to develop common integrated processors. A Westinghouse/Texas Instruments team was selected by both ATF teams to provide an airborne radar for the ATF demonstration and validation phase.

Boeing is responsible for offensive avionics and mission software. Martin-Marietta/General Electric is subcontractor, developing the Electro-Optic Sensor System (EOSS) for both the Lockheed YF-22 and Northrop YF-23 ATF prototypes. The ATF's EOSS, a wholly passive sensor system, will enhance ATF penetration into hostile airspace and will help the pilot evade hostile radar and air defenses.

Boeing is also developing an advanced ejector-seat/escape system, and a new flight G-suit for the pilot. The pilot of the ATF also might use a helmet-mounted weapon-aiming/aircraft status system, called AGILE EYE.

Boeing will integrate the radar and EOSS with the other avionics elements in the company's Integrated Technology Development Laboratory and will flight-test the systems in 1989 in a Boeing 757 flying testbed.

A goal of the ATF avionics development program is to achieve 90 percent commonality with the Navy's ATA avionics suite. Thus the new integrated electronic warfare system (INEWS) and integrated communication, navigation, and identification avionics (ICNIA) system, which are also slated for the ATA, will be a primary component of the ATF's avionics suite. An ultramodern fire control system and long-range, over-the-horizon phased-array radar are also planned for the ATF. This radar is capable of detecting targets that would normally be masked by the horizon, by bouncing radar energy off the ionosphere so that the radar energy can travel over the horizon.

For both the ATA and ATF, the Navy and Air Force consider the fighters' avionics packages to be a major challenge to fielding an effective ATA or ATF aircraft. Northrop's work on the phased-array radar is one of the reasons it was selected for the ATF program.

ATF Airframe Design

The goal for ATF design is not only to incorporate stealth technology for low-detectability signatures, but also to enable the ATF to cruise efficiently at Mach 1.5, carrying a full load of weapons, without having to use the full power output of the engines. Wing and fuselage blending, careful airfoil design, and conformal or internal weapons installation not only should keep RCS to a minimum, but should also make the design goal of part-throttle Mach 1.5 cruise possible. Composite materials also will be used in the ATF's airframe, as well as many other stealth techniques mentioned earlier.

With the capability of cruising at Mach 1.5 while not using too much fuel, the ATF should have a wide combat radius and the capability of being quickly sent to trouble spots, with enough fuel remaining to complete the mission and return to base. Light wing loading, high maximum lift coefficients, and a high thrust-to-weight ratio of 1.2 to 1 should give the ATF acceleration and a turn rate faster than that of the F-15 (FIG. 7-12) or of what might be the ATF's principal threats: the Soviet MiG-29 and Su-27 (FIGS. 7-13 and 7-14), or whatever future designs that are taking shape on Soviet drawing boards. The ATF's sustained turn rate at 35,000 feet and at supersonic speed, for example, should be 50 percent better than any existing or potential threat. Subsonic sustained turn rates should be 25 percent better than the F-15, and instantaneous turn rate should be 25 percent better, both supersonic and subsonic. At low altitudes, turn rates won't be much improved because the pilot can't endure loads of more than 9G's and it is far easier to pull high G-loads at lower altitudes than at higher altitudes.

Various flight-control systems are being considered for the ATF, including fly-by-wire and fly-by-light, and will be used to allow the ATF to be flown with excellent controllability on the edge of a stall or in other risky configurations. The computer-controlled electronic flight system allows the pilot to command, say, full up elevator, but will prevent the aircraft from stalling, thus making it possible for the pilot to

Fig. 7-12. The McDonnell Douglas F-15C Eagle fighter, due to be replaced by the advanced tactical fighter, is shown here with cluster bombs attached to the aircraft's Fast Packs on tangential pylons. (Courtesy McDonnell Douglas Corp.)

Fig. 7-13. A Soviet MiG-29 Fulcrum-A fighter interceptor carrying AA-8 Aphid infrared-guided missiles and AA-10 Alamo semiactive radar-guided missiles. The MiG-29 also employs an infrared search and track system (Nato coded EYEBALL*), mounted just to the right of the pilot's windscreen, and a track-while-scan air-to-air/air-to-ground radar with look-down capability. A one-barrel, 30-millimeter cannon is fitted in the port wing leading edge root extension. The Fulcrum-A has a high thrust-to-weight ratio and is highly maneuverable. While it might be a match for the F-15 Eagle or F-16, it will not be an effective counter to the new advanced tactical fighter. This is the main reason for development of the ATF.* (Courtesy Swedish Air Force)

Fig. 7-14. This Su-27 Flanker-B is yet another new fighter aircraft deployed by the Soviets. The Flanker is armed with three versions of the AA-10 Alamo air-to-air missile: those under the wings are infrared guided, while those under the air intake trunks and on the fuselage centerline are semiactive radar-guided types. The Flanker also has a 30-millimeter cannon in the starboard wing leading-edge root extension and the EYEBALL *infrared search and tracking system. Its radar is large and has search and tracking ranges greater than those of the F-15's radar, as well as look-down capability. With its high thrust-to-weight ratio (higher than the F-15), the Flanker is highly maneuverable and has speed and altitude capabilities similar to the F-15. The Flanker is also a reason development of the advanced tactical fighter is considered extremely important.* (Courtesy Royal Norwegian Air Force, photo by Number 333 Squadron.)

perform radical maneuvers without having to worry about flying out of one of the corners of the aircraft's performance envelope. Another benefit of electronic flight-control systems is that a highly maneuverable unstable aircraft, which would normally be impossible to fly by a human pilot, can be made to act stable by the computerized control system.

ATF Engines

Two engine companies are competing for the ATF powerplant contract. General Electric is offering a GE37 (USAF YF-120); Pratt & Whitney, a P&W 5000 (USAF YF-119). Both engines are turbofan types and will be in the 30,000-pound thrust class. The engines will feature modular construction, an advanced cooling design, and single-crystal turbine blades. Air Force specifications require the engines to be able to accept two-dimensional exhaust nozzles that can be vectored to provide variable-position and reverse thrust during flight and landing. The engines will have low bypass ratios and thrust-to-weight ratios of 10:1. They will be optimized for low specific fuel consumption at supersonic cruise speeds. The goal for reliability is an engine failure rate that is less than half that of current fighter engines. Line replacement units are to be easily accessible on the bottom of the engine. Prototype engines are running at both General Electric and Pratt & Whitney, and the companies' programs are on schedule.

Typical stealth techniques such as internal ducting, air intakes, and exhaust nozzles designed for reduced RCS, infrared, and acoustic signatures will be used for the ATF's engine installation. The 2-D exhaust nozzles, which can be moved to vector engine thrust in varying directions, combined with the MAW and close-coupled canards, should increase the ATF's combat maneuverability and allow short takeoff and landing distances. ATF specifications call for a 1,200-foot ground roll for takeoff and landing, which compares quite well with the lengthy 8,000 foot landing roll of the F-15.

While Northrop might take advantage of the 2-D nozzles for its version of the ATF, Lockheed isn't so sure about whether this kind of nozzle is advantageous and isn't planning to use the feature in its YF-22, although the 2-D nozzles will still be part of the engine.

According to a Lockheed official, "it's not an obvious thing, technically, because if you stop to think about it, you're going to fly at fairly high speeds, thus you're going to be at very high dynamic pressure, and what maneuverability you can get in the practical vector angles of thrust is going to turn out to be relatively small. Where it will be most helpful is at very low airspeeds. Now, the question concerns the cost and reliability in such a trade-off. Would you want to pay the weight penalty and the complexity and maintenance to thrust vector when maybe its principal contribution is in a speed range that you're not all that keen about in combat anyway? You may be able to maneuver much faster with an unstable aircraft outfitted with large control surfaces than with a relatively slow, heavy piece of engine machinery moving. Then you say at high speed, thrust vectoring won't contribute anything anyway, and the tradeoff might not be all that beneficial. Variable engine inlets that could improve the top speed of the ATF by several tenths of Mach number may also be excluded for cost and maintainability reasons.''

ATF program managers are aiming for extended range at high cruise speeds, which means the engines will need to be able to push the ATF at supersonic speeds without using afterburners. Even with fuel-efficient engines, the ATF will still have to carry a large amount of fuel internally—more so than comparable aircraft types. Using weight-saving composite materials for airframe construction should allow the required fuel to be carried without the need for externally mounted, expendable fuel tanks (drop tanks). In-flight refueling will be used for the ATF, but long-range capability on its own fuel supply is still desired.

Northrop and Lockheed are allowed to choose either engine for their two ATF prototypes, or they might decide to install GE engines in one prototype and P&W engines in the other.

ATF Weapons

Conventional weapons, such as the AIM-7 Sparrow and AIM-9 Sidewinder missiles and a 20-mm gatling gun, will be used on the ATF. Newer weapons under development also will be used, including the AIM-120 AMRAAM active-radar guided AAM, the AIM 132 ASRAAM infrared-guided AAM, and the new advanced air-to-air missile (AAAM) being developed by the Navy.

Ford Aerospace has developed a number of midcaliber advanced ammunition concepts such as telescoped 20-mm designs for the Air Force's advanced technology gun (ATG). Its round has the same muzzle velocity and kinetic impact of a 25-mm round. Advanced development has been accomplished on a 25-mm design as well. Telescoped ammunition enables reduced systems size and power requirements, and is easier to handle and smaller than conventional ammunition.

Ford Aerospace is developing advanced air-defense, antiarmor, and multipurpose combat projectiles. The company's maneuvering projectiles have been developed and successfully demonstrated. Ford's advanced electro-optical targeting pod (Nite Owl), which incorporates a laser target designator/ranger (LTD/R), can be adapted to the ATF and ATA.

Operational ATF

The ATF is designed to engage long-range targets as opposed to nearby targets. It will be a first-see, first-shoot fighter, designed to destroy hostile targets long before the ATF pilot visually spots the threat. The ATF will be extremely versatile, however, and should be able to outmaneuver any aircraft in the sky today or in the year 2000 and be so stealthy that hostile aircraft will be unable to obtain the infrared or radar lock-on needed to engage and destroy the ATF. An enemy pilot's best hope against the ATF would probably be a gunshot, but this would only be possible if the enemy were able to maneuver directly behind the agile ATF.

Some observers feel the ATF is the last fighter aircraft, but it would be wise not to bet on that assumption. In its Forecast II studies, the Air Force envisions aerospacecraft the size of the F-15 that will be able to take off from normal runways and fly directly to Earth orbit. Outside the atmosphere, this craft could engage either orbital targets or "fly" to another location, reenter the atmosphere, and destroy a hostile target. It would then rendezvous with a tanker, return to orbit, and return to and land at home base. Thus, the ATF might be the last fighter of this century and it might be the last traditional fighter aircraft, but it will definitely not be the last word in fighter-combat flying vehicles.

The Air Force is urging its European allies in the NATO community and non-NATO members Japan and Israel to join in the development of the ATF. The Air Force feels that the European fighter aircraft (EAP), which should lead to a European combat aircraft, as well as the French Rafale, Sweden's JAS 39 Grippen, and Israel's canceled Lavi would not be capable of defeating new Soviet fighters such as the MiG-29 Fulcrum or Su-27 Flanker or two newer types—including one that is similar to the ATF—that might be under development.

Japan had a proposed fighter project called FS-X that was intended to include stealth technology similar to that of the ATF program. Japan's Mitsubishi, lead contractor in the FS-X program, developed computer programs to determine RCS of various FS-X design features and codeveloped RAM that may be used for the FS-X. This research was done at Mitsubishi's Komaki South factory in a specially designed radio-frequency absorbing anechoic chamber.

Chapter Eight

Helicopters and V/STOL Aircraft with Some Stealth Features

THE FOLLOWING ARE HELICOPTERS AND V/STOL (VERTICAL OR SHORT takeoff or landing) aircraft that have some stealth features or that are specifically intended for stealth missions.

Helicopters and V/STOL Aircraft	Status
Sikorsky AARV	Canceled
McDonnell Douglas MH-6	Operational
Phalanx Dragon	Under development
Bell D292 ACAP	Test Only
Sikorsky S-75 ACAP	Test Only
Bell/McDonnell Douglas LHX	Under development
Boeing/Sikorsky LHX	Under development

SIKORSKY AARV

FIGURE 8-1 shows a helicopter proposed by Sikorsky to fit an early 1970s requirement of the U.S. Army for an armored aerial reconnaissance vehicle (AARV). Sikorsky's proposal has an ideal shape for a stealth helicopter, with many flat, angled external surfaces that would absorb or scatter radar energy, and a low profile in general.

In firing tests on a mockup of Sikorsky's AARV, .30-caliber ball and armor-piercing rounds failed to pierce the mockup's structure. If Sikorsky had built this helicopter using RAM, it might have been a perfect candidate for the Army's current LIGHT, HELICOPTER, EXPERIMENTAL (LHX) PROGRAM.

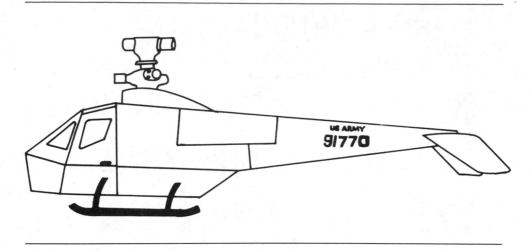

Fig. 8-1. Early 1970s proposal by Sikorsky for Army's armored aerial reconnaissance vehicle program. It featured angled, flat external surfaces that would have absorbed and dissipated radar energy.

Design features included dual counterrotating main rotors that eliminate the need for a noisy and vulnerable tail rotor, an inverted V-tail stabilizer, and a Pratt & Whitney Canada PT-6 turboshaft engine. Easy access to critical systems for simplified maintenance was made possible by the low stance of the helicopter, allowing the ground crew to work on the engine without climbing on stools or ladders.

The AARV program was canceled, but some of its features have been resurrected in the design of Sikorsky's S-75 advanced composite airframe program (ACAP) helicopter.

Another black helicopter program might be underway at Sikorsky. In 1985, it was reported that Sikorsky was developing a stealth helicopter under contract to DARPA and the U.S. Army. This contract is presumed to be separate from Sikorsky's S-75 ACAP and LHX programs, though little more has been revealed and the existence of the program is still in doubt.

MCDONNELL DOUGLAS MH-6

The MH-6 is a modified version of the Army/McDonnell Douglas Helicopter Co. OH-6 Cayuse observation helicopter. Work done to reduce detectability signatures of the MH-6 includes modifications to the engine and main rotor to suppress infrared and acoustic signatures. The modifications reportedly make the MH-6 one of the quietest helicopters in the world, capable of hovering a few hundred feet from a person without being heard by that person. Both members of the two-man crew use night-vision goggles and FLIR systems, enabling them to fly the MH-6 at top speed just above tree level in the middle of the night. The MH-6 is small enough to be carried in most Air Force transport planes to trouble spots that require the services of this unique helicopter.

The MH-6 is equipped with 7.62 -mm mini machine-gun pods and 2.75-inch rocket pods. It was first operated by the CIA, but now the Army's Task Force 160 of the Special Operations Forces in Ft. Bragg, North Carolina, operates 30 MH-6s. American military forces used the MH-6 during the invasion of Grenada in 1980, and it has also seen action in Central America in support of American-backed Contra rebels fighting along the Honduras/Nicaragua border.

The Army/Bell OH-58D AHIP helicopter performs a mission similar to that of the MH-6.

PHALANX DRAGON

Little is known about the Dragon (FIG. 8-2), especially whether or not it will actually fly. It looks somewhat like an aircraft that would be at home in the pages of a superhero comic book, rather than an aircraft that could be a major stealth weapon.

The Dragon could be a competitor to the LHX, if allowed to compete in the program. It is being designed by a company called Phalanx Organization, Inc. based in Long Beach, California, and is a vertical takeoff and landing (VTOL) aircraft. Its shape and the materials that might be used in its construction make it an ideal candidate for low-observable requirements.

The powertrain of the Phalanx Dragon was scheduled for pylon testing in late 1987. According to Phalanx Organization CEO Bill Moody, two single-engine

Fig. 8-2. Drawing of a conceptual mockup of the Phalanx Dragon VTOL combat aircraft.

demonstrator VTOL aircraft are under construction at Phalanx's Long Beach head-quarters. They will be used to verify and flight-test the Dragon's technology and pave the way for the twin-engine MP-21 that eventually will be offered for sale. The components used on the pylon test rig are designed to fit into the MP-21, thus saving a step in construction and bringing the MP-21 up to operational speed somewhat faster. The MP-21 airframe is also under construction at present, Moody said.

Performance of the MP-21 includes 650-knot maximum speed, 30- to 40-knot reverse speed, 2,400- to 2,600-nautical-mile range carrying normal fuel of about 1,800 pounds, and maximum takeoff weight of 10,000 pounds. Seating will be available for either one, two, or three people, depending on buyer specifications. Three crewmembers might be needed, Moody noted, because of air-to-air combat requirements that specify a rear-facing gunner. Both the demonstrators and the MP-21 will be powered by 4,500- to 5,000-pound Garrett 731-3 turbine engines.

Each engine will power two thrust nozzles, similar to those used on the VTOL Harrier jumpjet. There are eight thrust nozzles altogether: four used for horizontal flight, and four for vertical flight. Only four nozzles are used at a time, and if one engine fails, no adverse yaw or roll will result because each engine thrusts through two nozzles, one on each side of the airframe. The left engine, for instance, delivers its power to one horizontal or one vertical nozzle on the left side and the same on the right. Single-engine flight also will be possible.

The MP-21 will be able to continue to fly horizontally even if the the vertical nozzles have been destroyed by enemy artillery, although it would not be able to hover, Moody explained. Conventional control surfaces—aileron, rudder, and elevator—are also part of the airframe, and were added, Moody said, by popular demand. Low fuel consumption—a projected .485 pounds per pound per hour—is maintained by varying the size of the nozzles' outlets to keep the proper 1,100- to 1,200-foot-per-second exhaust velocity for maximum efficiency, Moody explained.

U.S. ARMY ADVANCED COMPOSITE AIRFRAME PROGRAM

Bell Helicopter Textron and Sikorsky Aircraft are participating in an Army contract for development and production assessment of a helicopter airframe made primarily of composite materials, called the ADVANCED COMPOSITE AIRFRAME PROGRAM (ACAP). Objectives of the program were an airframe 22 percent lighter and 17 percent less expensive than a similar metal airframe. Also expected as a result of the ACAP are improved military helicopter characteristics using composites such as Kevlar, graphite, and Fiberglas; survivability in a 42-foot-per-second vertical crash; and reduced radar signature.

The program is being conducted in two phases; first, engineering design and design support testing; and second, construction and testing of three airframes; one tool-proofing article confined to ballistic-tolerance testing, one flight test article to be ground tested for 15 hours and flight-tested for 50 hours, and one static test airframe.

Fig. 8-3. Bell/Army D292 advanced composite airframe program (ACAP) helicopter during test flights. (Courtesy Bell Helicopter TEXTRON)

Bell Model D292 ACAP

Bell earned a $37 million contract as its part of the ACAP. The D292 design is based on Bell's commercial 222 helicopter and uses the same engine, transmission, and rotor system (FIG. 8-3). Grumman Aerospace built 30 percent of the airframe, and Menasco Inc. provided the landing gear, which was of the fixed type.

Fuselage beams, frames, bulkheads, and the forward roof are made of graphite to provide stiffness. The fuselage shell, nose, canopy frame, vertical fin, horizontal stabilizer, and fuel compartment bulkhead and flooring are made of Kevlar. The tailboom skin and cargo door are made of Fiberglas. The firewall is made of Nextel polymide. The rear cabin roof is made of graphite and Fiberglas/bismalimide composite. All these composite materials bring the maximum takeoff weight of the D292 down to 7,500 pounds, compared to the 222's maximum takeoff weight of 8,250 pounds.

Sikorsky S-75 ACAP

Sikorsky's share of the ACAP contract was $17 million, awarded in 1981 for construction of an all-composite helicopter airframe. Two Allison 250-C30 engines and the rotor system and drivetrain from a Sikorsky S-76 were used in Sikorsky's ACAP airframe. The result was a 24 percent reduction in weight and 23 percent reduction in cost. The airframe easily met the Army's goals, including those of crashworthiness, ballistic tolerance, reliability and maintainability, and radar signature

Fig. 8-4. Sikorsky S-75 advanced composite airframe program (ACAP) helicopter. (Courtesy Sikorsky)

reduction. Some of Sikorsky's earlier work on the AARV found its way into the S-75 (FIG. 8-4), namely the angled flat fuselage side panels that helped reduce radar signature. Landing gear was fixed.

Subcontractors on the program were LTV Corp., which built the airframe's lower tub section, and Hercules Corp., which built the tailcone, tail pylon, and stabilizer. Sikorsky was responsible for final assembly and fabrication of the rest of the components that made up the airframe.

Sikorsky S-75 ACAP Specifications

Overall length	52 ft 5 in, rotors turning
Fuselage length	43 ft 6 in
Fuselage width	8 ft
Height	14 ft 9 in
Wheelbase	17 ft 3 in
Gear track	9 ft 5 in
Rotor diameter	44 ft
Tail rotor diameter	8 ft
Crew	pilot and copilot
Passengers	six combat-equipped troops
Maximum takeoff weight	8,470 lb
Empty weight	5,944 lb
Maximum speed	173.8 mph
Endurance	2.3 hr

U.S. ARMY LIGHT HELICOPTER EXPERIMENTAL PROGRAM

The LIGHT HELICOPTER EXPERIMENTAL (LHX) program, as originally planned was a multibillion dollar plan designed to replace the Bell UH-1 (Huey) Series and Bell's AH-1S and OH-58D AHIP scout helicopters with a more survivable and capable light helicopter. The Army had said it wanted to buy 4,535 LHXs in two versions based on a single design: 2,127 LHX-SCATs (scout/attack, FIG. 8-5), of which 1,100 would be attack versions and 1,027 scout versions, each priced at no more than $8 million, and the LHX-U (utility), now abandoned, would have cost $5 million (FIG. 8-6).

The SCAT will be a twin-engine fighter helicopter designed for a single pilot, while the utility version will have a two-man crew and be able to carry six to eight combat troops. A number of radical helicopter concepts were studied and proposed by American helicopter manufacturers, including tilt-rotor designs, the X-wing, and counterrotating rotors, but a conventional single-rotor design was selected by the Army for further development.

Stealth capability via low radar, infrared, visual, and acoustic signatures is to be a major goal for the LHX program, and technology developed in the ACAP and AD-VANCED ROTOR TECHNOLOGY INTEGRATION (ARTI) programs will be applied to make the LHX stealthy.

Fig. 8-5. Three-view drawing of the Bell/McDonnell Douglas revised version of the LHX helicopter. (Courtesy McDonnell Douglas Helicopter Co.)

Fig. 8-6. Artist's impression of a Bell/McDonnell Douglas LHX utility version. (Courtesy Bell Helicopter TEXTRON)

The two LHX versions will carry different weapons: LHX-SCAT likely will sport a heavy-caliber chin-mounted gun that can be aimed by the pilot's helmet sights and that is tied into the day/night sensor package. Other weapons might include the Hellfire ASM and Stinger AAM mounted internally in swing-out launchers or conformal firing ports. All flying and weapons systems will be nearly fully automated to reduce pilot workload.

The planned LHX-U's missions were geared more toward rescue and casevac (casualty evacuation) or internal and external (sling) cargo carrying so no armament beyond a light machine gun mounted on a swivel in the passenger doorway will be required. Landing gear will be retractable for added aerodynamic cleanliness of the airframe.

Three contractor teams are working on the T800 advanced turboprop engine slated for the LHX: Allison/Garrett, Avco Lycoming/Pratt & Whitney, and General Electric/Williams International. Output of the T800 will be 1,200 shaft horsepower, and the two mounted in the LHX will provide 2,400 total shaft horsepower for the nimble stealthy helicopter.

Two contractor teams—Boeing/Sikorsky and Bell/McDonnell Douglas—have been awarded contracts to build two prototype LHXs that should fly in the early 1990s. Initial operational capability for LHX should occur in 1996.

Bell/McDonnell Douglas LHX

The Bell/McDonnell Douglas LHX features flush engine air intakes, a conformal exhaust nozzle with low infrared and acoustic signatures, and a low-RCS fuselage made of RAM with a sleek, wedge-shaped cockpit. Instead of a conventional tail rotor, this team's LHX might use either a shrouded tail rotor, which is much quieter than unshrouded tail rotors, or McDonnell Douglas's proven Notar (no tail rotor) design.

Notar consists of a tail boom through which air is vented under pressure to steer the helicopter in yaw. McDonnell Douglas has tested a Notar-configured MD500 helicopter extensively, and the design has proven to be extremely quiet, maneuverable, and safe. During demonstrations of the Notar MD500, pilots have purposely approached trees in the helicopter and forced the craft's tailboom into the branches to show how much less vulnerable the Notar helicopter is to tail-rotor strikes. McDonnell Douglas is currently designing a commercial Notar-equipped helicopter, and the design could certainly have many military applications, especially for stealth missions.

Boeing/Sikorsky LHX

The Boeing/Sikorsky team is taking similar steps with its LHX as far as fuselage design for low detectability signature is concerned, including flush engine air intakes and conformal exhaust nozzles (FIGS. 8-7 and 8-8). A shrouded tail rotor, where the tail rotor blades are surrounded by the vertical fin for additional thrust and quieter operation, is planned for Boeing/Sikorsky's LHX.

The Boeing/Sikorsky LHX *First Team* (The McDonnell Douglas/Bell team is known as the *Super Team*) has unveiled a powered ¹⁄₁₂-scale model of its preliminary design of the LHX for the U.S. Army's next generation of light-attack/armed reconnaissance

Fig. 8-7. The Boeing/Sikorsky team's proposed LHX-SCAT (light helicopter exprimental, scout/attack). (Courtesy Boeing Helicopter)

Fig. 8-8. The Boeing/Sikorsky team's proposed light helicopter experimental utility helicopter (LHX-U). (Courtesy Sikorsky)

helicopters. Boeing/Sikorsky also discussed elements of the team's Demonstration/Validation (Dem/Val) phase strategy and announced some changes in the team's composition.

Distinguishing features of the design include a T-tail with fan-in-tail rotor; internal missile bays that maintain clean aerodynamic and low-observable lines; a turreted gun that can be slewed by the pilot's head movements; a tandem two-seat cockpit allowing the helicopter to be flown by one or two people. The flight controls feature fiberoptical links (fly-by-light) to carry the control inputs. They are immune to electromagnetic interference, and were developed in the Boeing/Army ADVANCED DIGITAL OPTICAL CONTROL SYSTEM (ADOCS) program.

Other features of the design include an all-composite (radar absorbent/transparent materials) airframe and a five-blade main rotor with swept tips. In every sense of the word, the LHX designs from both contractor teams are stealth helicopters.

The LHX's engines are to be twin turboshafts, rated at 1200 shp each. Teams that competed for the engine contract included Textron Lycoming/Pratt & Whitney and Allison/Garrett LHTEC. The Allison/Garrett team won the contract in early November 1988. The LHX engine is designated the T800 by the Army.

The configuration is the baseline design the *First Team* presented to the Army in their Dem/Val proposal, submitted September 9, 1988. A number of validation and trade studies will be conducted on the airframe and electronic mission equipment package (MEP) during the 18-month Dem/Val phase to ensure the Boeing/Sikorsky design is the best one to take a full-scale development.

Lou Cotton, Boeing Sikorsky LHX program manager, expressed confidence in the team's approach to LHX design and development. "Since the time our team was formed, we have been convinced that our advanced technology helicopter airframe concept would best meet the Army's requirements. Subsequent independent studies have borne that out," Cotton said.

Cotton emphasized the strengths Boeing/Sikorsky team members bring to the program. "This team is a Who's Who of the aerospace, electronics, and defense industries. In aggregate, we have worked on nearly every current major defense aviation program, including UH-60, CH-47, AH-64, and AH-1 helicopters, the FB-111, B-52, and B-1B bombers, the V-22 tilt-rotor, and F-14, F-15, F-16, F-18, A-10, AV-8, ATA and ATF fighters.

"The LHX challenge is a technology integration and program management challenge. Our team members have been instrumental in developing and/or building some of the most advanced weapons systems in the world. We're capitalizing on the unmatched know-how to develop and build the LHX," Cotton said.

Noting that the MEP integration is one of the most demanding LHX tasks, Cotton made particular mention of the team's avionics system integrator, Boeing Military Airplanes.

"Boeing Military Airplanes has done incredibly complex work integrating the B-52 bomber upgrade program, and their work on the offensive avionics on the B-1B is probably the most sophisticated systems integration work ever done. The offensive systems on the airplane are outstanding.

"Throughout the past three years we have been conducting internal competitions among our team members to sharpen our team's competitive edge. As a result we have made some changes in the makeup and assignments of the Boeing Sikorsky team. General Electric of Burlington, Vermont, has been added to develop the turreted gun system. Martin Marietta will have total responsibility for the electro-optic (EO) systems. Link simulation will be responsible for operator training systems, and a team of Westinghouse and TRW supported by AT&T will provide both the signal and data processors. TRW and Westinghouse working together will develop the Aircraft Survivability Equipment."

The avionic systems of the LHX (of both contractor teams) are to be compatible with avionic systems found on the ATA and ATF combat aircraft.

The next step for the LHX program is the Dem/Val phase, expected to have begun in late 1988. As presently scheduled, the phase will last through April 1990. A five-year full-scale-development phase will begin in December 1990, with LHX initial operational capability (IOC) planned for 1996. Production run for the LHX is anticipated through 2005. Unit fly-away cost projected for each LHX is $7.5 million.

The U.S. Army's next-generation LHX helicopter might not be as fast (top flight speed) as the Soviet Hokum fighter-helicopter, but the LHX will be more advanced in terms of rotary-wing technology, as well as have more stealth features than the Hokum. This last feature, stealth, might make all the difference in the world when, or even if the LHX meets the Hokum in air combat.

LHX Required Specifications

Empty weight	7,500 lb
Maximum takeoff weight	11,000 lb
Maximum flight speed	196 mph
Cruise speed	184 mph
Armament	Typical mission: One 20 mm, rotary chin-mounted, turreted gun; other weapons internally mounted, and can include eight Hellfire multirole missile, two Stinger air-to-air missiles. Ammunition for the 20 mm gun is 500 rounds. On this type of mission, the LHX will have 1.8 hour of internal fuel.

OTHER HELICOPTERS

Boeing has flown and is currently testing its all-composite Model 360 twin-tandem-rotor helicopter (FIG. 8-9). This model could have some stealth applications because of its low radar, noise, and infrared signatures.

Fig. 8-9. *Boeing Vertol Model 360 composite helicopter. This helicopter, although not specifically intended for stealth missions, could have excellent stealth capabilities because of its composite airframe and specially designed engine intake and exhaust systems.* (Courtesy Boeing Helicopters)

Fig. 8-10. Artist's concept of the Bell/Boeing V-22 Osprey tilt-rotor aircraft. This aircraft could have stealth applications because its airframe is made of composite materials and its engine exhaust system is designed to reduce the craft's infrared signature. The first V-22 was rolled out May 23, 1988. (Courtesy Boeing Helicopters)

The Bell/Boeing V-22 Osprey tilt-rotor aircraft, which takes off vertically then transitions into fast forward flight by tilting its engines and rotor/prop blades forward after takeoff, is also made almost entirely of composite materials (FIG. 8-10). The V-22 should be extremely quiet based on tests conducted with NASA's XV-15 tilt-rotor technology demonstrator, and it might end up being a capable, stealthy aircraft.

The first V-22 was rolled out of Bell's Arlington, Texas factory on May 23, 1988. The tri-service V-22 Osprey tilt-rotor prototype's first flight date was scheduled to be mid-August 1988. This target date for the V-22 was not achieved, because pre-flight tests showed minor problems with the integration of some flight systems. First flight was rescheduled for November-December 1988 because of these delays.

Performance of the V-22 includes the ability to carry 24 fully equipped combat troops or 10,000 to 15,000 pounds of cargo. Top speed is projected to be 300 knots, and range 500 nautical miles.

Chapter Nine

Unmanned Stealth Aircraft

UNMANNED AIR VEHICLES (UAVs), USUALLY REMOTELY PILOTED VEHICLES (RPVs), are excellent candidates for stealth technology, and much stealth research and effort has been done on these aircraft. Those listed in this chapter use stealth technology extensively. Although there are many more models than there is room to describe here, the following should serve as a good example of how extensively stealth technology is being used in the United States.

Unmanned Stealth Aircraft	Status
THAP	Feasibility study
Lockheed GTD-21 Senior Bowl	No longer operational
Teledyne drones	Some operational
Teledyne AQM-91 Compass Arrow	No longer operational
LTV/E-Systems XQM-93 Compass Dwell	Test Only
Boeing YQM-94 Compass Cope B-Gull	Test only, canceled
Teledyne YQM-98 Compass Cope R-Tern	Test only
Airforce ARPV	
Lockheed MQM-105 Aquila	Operational
U.S. Army CM-30	Development testing
U.S. Army CM-44	Under development
Boeing/DARPA Teal Cameo	Under development
Leading Systems/Amber	Under development

TACTICAL HIGH-ALTITUDE PENETRATOR

The Tactical High-Altitude Penetrator (THAP) looks like the Benson/AMR/Ryan RPV-007 design. FIGURE 9-1 shows a drawing based on the THAP concept. The concept resulted from a study for a tactical high-altitude penetrator design, which is a UAV that can carry a weapons payload in an internal weapons bay.

The aircraft's thrust would have been provided by two high-technology turbofan engines mounted on the top of the airframe. The engines would have some components made of RAM. The airframe shape was the span-loaded flying-wing type and would rest on a tricycle landing gear. Pitch, yaw, and roll control would have been provided by two vertical fins canted inward, and called *rudderatorons*. The materials making up the airframe were to include RAM plastics surrounding a foam core.

THAP is now believed to have been related to Northrop's B-2's proof-of-concept vehicles, and also to the Tactical Stealth Aircraft (TSA) program. THAP is thought to have been built by Northrop, and test-flown from Groom Lake flight test facility on the Nellis Air Force range since 1983.

LOCKHEED MISSILES AND SPACE GTD-21B SENIOR BOWL

The D-21, dubbed PROJECT SENIOR BOWL, was a Mach 4 reconnaissance RPV designed jointly by Lockheed Missiles and Space and Lockheed's Skunkworks, designed

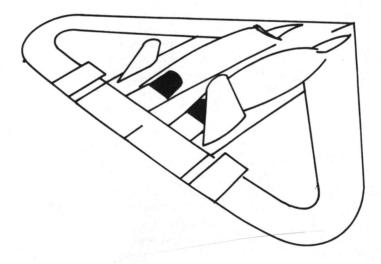

Fig. 9-1. A tactical high-altitude penetrator concept, based on a design study.

to be launched from Lockheed's A-12 and flown over territory that was considered too risky for the manned A-12. Data obtained by the D-21 was relayed either to the A-12 (called MOTHER GOOSE during these missions) or to a nearby ground station.

Construction was of Lockheed-developed heat-resistant plastics and RAM, and its shape was designed for low RCS. Wing planform was similar to that of the speedy A-12, but it had only one powerplant, a single low-detectability signature Marquardt RJ43-MA-11 ramjet engine, and one vertical fin. Engine air intake design used the same automatic translating spike design as the A-12.

Only 38 D-21s were built, and 20 were lost during the drone's short service life. For launching from the A-12, the D-21 was carried on an aft dorsal fuselage pylon, but during most of the D-21's operational missions, it was launched from two B-52H bombers modified for D-21 launches.

On the B-52H, two D-21s were carried on the in-board external pylons under the bomber's wings, and for these launches a boost rocket engine with its own fuel tank was mounted beneath the D-21. After launching, the boost engine accelerated the D-21 to about Mach 2.5, at which speed the drone's own ramjet engine could take over and push the drone up its Mach 4 cruising speed. During most of its missions, the D-21 cruised over 100,000 feet.

The U.S. Air Force's 4200th Test Wing at Beale AFB in California was the operational B-52H/D-21 unit, although the most valuable D-21 reconnaissance flights were accomplished from bases where the B-52Hs were assigned on temporary duty.

The D-21's lack of success when launched from the A-12 might have been because many accidents occurred during launching. Two A-12s were modified to launch the D-21, but one was lost during a test launching of a D-21 from the aft dorsal pylon that is installed between the A-12's vertical fins. To keep the D-21 from slowing down its host A-12, and aerodynamic fairing covered the D-21's ramjet air inlet when the drone was being carried.

D-21 Drone Specifications

Length	43 ft, 2 in
Wingspan	19 ft
Maximum weight	About 20,000 lb

TELEDYNE RYAN AERONAUTICAL Q-2 AND MODEL 147

The U.S. Air Force has operated many versions of the so-called lightning bug RPVs or UAVs. The term *lightning bug* comes from the vehicles' insectlike appearance, with skinny wings and underslung engines (FIG. 9-2). One series of these UAVs were pioneers in the use of stealth technology for remote reconnaissance: Teledyne Ryan Aeronautical's Model 147T/TE/TF, and the Q-2 and Q-2C.

Original versions of these UAVs had RAM blankets added to the airframe, while later versions were built of RAM and had low RCS values. A wire mesh smaller than the wavelength of typical military radars was installed over the engine air intake to prevent incoming radar energy from entering the air intake and reflecting off the

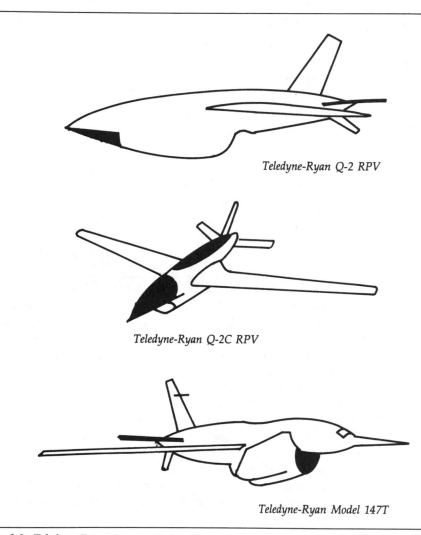

Teledyne-Ryan Q-2 RPV

Teledyne-Ryan Q-2C RPV

Teledyne-Ryan Model 147T

Fig. 9-2. Teledyne Ryan Aeronautical unmanned air vehicles or remotely piloted vehicles.

engine compressor. The 147T was built from the ground up as a stealth vehicle, rather than with add-on stealth materials, with what was called high-absorbency integrated defenses (HIDE).

These reconnaissance UAVs served in the Vietnam War and over China, and gathered valuable intelligence information. They were air-launched from modified C-130s. After completing its mission, the UAV would pop a parachute, then be snatched in midair by a team in a Sikorsky H-53 helicopter.

Many of these UAVs were lost in Vietnam and China, but they were probably drones that hadn't received the full stealth treatment. Those that took full advantage of the available stealth technology presented difficult radar targets fro both Vietnamese and Chinese air defenses, although it has been reported that during testing, some Q-2s could be successfully intercepted by Air Force F-106 fighters.

Q-2 UAV Specifications

Length	22 ft, 10 in
Body diameter	3 ft, 1 in
Wingspan	12 ft, 10 in
Wing area	36 sq ft
Maximum weight	2,500 lb
Maximum speed	690 mph
Cruise speed	630 mph
Ceiling	60,000 ft
Range	692 mi
Endurance	1 hr 15 min
Powerplant	One Teledyne CAE J69-T29 turbojet rated at 1,700 lb

TELEDYNE RYAN AERONAUTICAL MODEL 154 COMPASS ARROW AND AQM-91A FIREFLY

The Model 154 was the first large-scale UAV to use stealth technology for survival against hostile air defenses and was based on an earlier Teledyne Ryan UAV proposal known as RED WAGON, or Model 136. REDWAGON was proposed to the Air Force as a stealthy high-altitude reconnaissance UAV, but never made it to the hardware stage.

In addition to being made from RAM, the Model 154 had an almost perfectly flat belly and an engine with its exhaust on top of the fuselage, giving the vehicle extremely low radar and infrared signatures (FIG. 9-3). The Model 154 had long-span slightly swept wings mounted near the bottom of the fuselage for efficient high-altitude flight to keep it above most air defenses. The empennage consisted of twin vertical fins at the ends of the horizontal stabilizer.

Launch and recovery was similar to that of the Model 147, with launch from a C-130 and mid-air recovery by helicopter. Like the Model 147, the Model 154 was used extensively over China and Vietnam.

Teledyne Ryan's AQM-91A, or Firefly, competed against a Rockwell UAV concept in 1966 and was selected by the U.S. Air Force. The AQM-91A's mission equipment included infrared and optical sensors and Elint equipment.

The remaining Model 154 and AQM-91A UAVs are currently in storage.

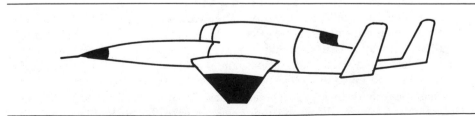

Fig. 9-3. Teledyne Ryan Aeronautical AQM-91A Compass Arrow UAV.

Rollout of the B-2 Bomber was held November 22, 1988, at the Palmdale, California, airport.

This artist's concept of the B-2 was released before any official photographs. As you can see, this rendering is very similar to the actual aircraft.

Artist's concept of the Boeing/Sikorsky LHX helicopter.

An advanced vertical take-off and landing air vehicle, with stealth qualities. This is a concept for a single-seat, X-wing/rotary-wing vehicle.

Lockheed-California Company's Advanced Tactical Fighter (ATF) will be able to dominate any hostile skies of the early twenty-first century.

Advanced flight station technologies pictured in this artist's concept represent many being developed by Lockheed for integration into its design for the ATF.

This ATF concept, shown here in model form, is similar to one once studied by McDonnell Douglas.

The F-117A has been operational since October 1983 and is assigned to the 4450th Tactical Group at Nellis AFB, Nevada.

Model 154 Specifications

Length	43 ft
Body diameter	3 ft, 2.25 in
Powerplant	One 5,270-lb GE J97 turbojet

LTV/E-SYSTEMS L450F/XQM-93 COMPASS DWELL

LTV's L450F (FIGS. 9-4 and 9-5) first flew, as a manned vehicle, in February 1970, although the vehicle was intended to be an unmanned long-endurance high-altitude reconnaissance vehicle. Stealth materials gave the L450F excellent low-observable characteristics. Suppression of radar and infrared signatures was a major goal of the program.

In addition to excellent stealth characteristics, the L450F also was quiet and had long endurance. The airframe, like that of Lockheed's QT-2 and Q-Star, was based on Schweizer's SGS 2-32 sailplane. It had a 475-shaft horsepower PWC PT6A-34 turboprop engine driving a three-blade Hartzell propeller.

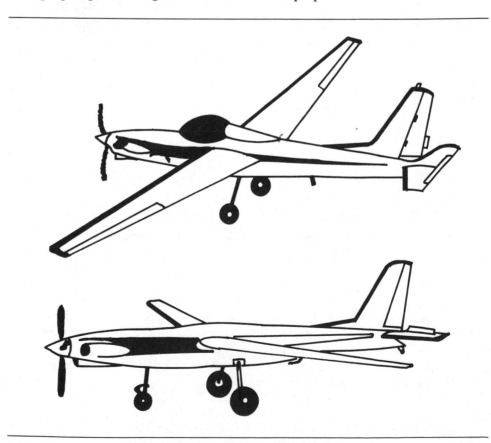

Fig. 9-4. (top) Manned version of the LTV/E-Systems L450F/XQM-93 Compass Dwell high-altitude reconnaissance aircraft. (bottom) Unmanned version of the L450F.

Fig. 9-5. L450F UAV in Air Force markings.

The second prototype flew as an unmanned vehicle and was evaluated by the Air Force at Edwards AFB under the COMPASS DWELL PROGRAM as military designation XQM-93. A competing design from Martin Marietta was evaluated alongside the L450F. The Air Force's COMPASS DWELL evaluation ended in early 1972, and neither the L450F nor Martin Marietta's competing UAV were selected for service.

L450F Specifications

Length	29 ft, 7 in
Height	10 ft, 8 in
Wingspan	57 ft
Maximum weight	4,600 lb manned
	5,300 lb unmanned
Payload	1,100 lb
Cruise speed	105 mph
Glide ratio	28:1
Endurance	24 hr plus

BOEING B-GULL/YQM-94A COMPASS COPE

The U.S. Air Force selected Boeing's B-Gull, designated YQM-94A, in the COMPASS COPE UAV competition, but the B-Gull was canceled and Lockheed's manned TR-1 was used instead. Teledyne Ryan Aeronautical's R-Tern YQM-98A was a competitor in the bid for the contract (FIG. 9-6).

The B-Gull (FIGS. 9-7 and 9-8) was a high-altitude, long-endurance UAV designed as a multipurpose sensor platform for a variety of battlefield support missions. The feasibility of the COMPASS COPE concept was proven during the prototype B-Gull's testing program, but the follow-up program that was to have tested and verified the B-Gull's reliable all-weather capability, multipurpose mission performance, and cost effectiveness was canceled in 1979.

The B-Gull's landing gear was retractable, and its engine—a General Electric J97 turbojet in the prototype—was mounted above the fuselage. If the B-Gull had gone into production, its engine would have been a Garret TFE 731 turbofan. Flight tests of the prototype B-Gull verified the design's structural integrity and handling characteristics, and no major configuration or structural design changes were planned

Fig. 9-6. Teledyne Ryan Aeronautical Model 235 YQM-98A Compass Cope R-Tern unmanned air vehicle. (Courtesy U.S. Air Force)

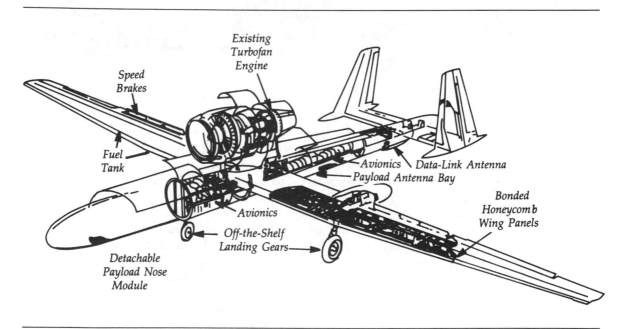

Fig. 9-7. Boeing B-Gull configuration and layout of internal systems.

for the production version. The radar-transparent Fiberglas fuselage had more than 40 cubic feet of space for internal antennas; over 100 cubic feet in the nose were available for payload-related equipment. The bonded honeycomb wing carried fuel from tip to tip in leakproof tanks, and the wing's computer-optimized laminar airfoil gave the B-Gull a lift-to-drag ratio greater than that of many sailplanes.

Major design goals for the Compass Cope UAV were that it be highly versatile and capable of a variety of surveillance missions. The B-Gull fulfilled these requirements with unique design features that gave it multimission flexibility. The B-Gull's nose was detachable to accommodate up to 26 different payloads, and the

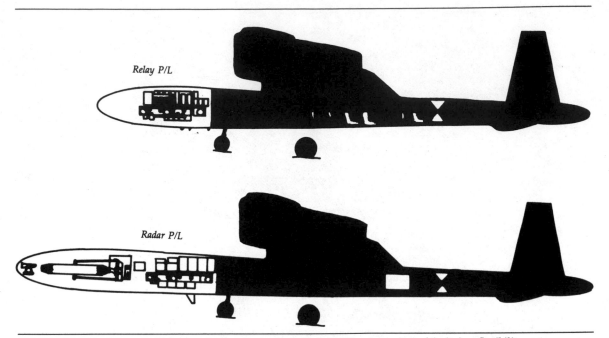

Fig. 9-8. Various noses could be attached to Boeing's B-Gull UAV, giving it multimission flexibility.

various payloads could be carried without major airframe redesign. The Fiberglas radome permitted 360-degree electronic surveillance from antennas mounted inside the radome. An automatic flight-control system was to be used throughout each flight for safe all-weather operation, and this system featured redundant digital computers, an automatic return-to-base mode, and a reliable control link. The automatic system was to have been used continuously, monitored by a human pilot who would observe the B-Gull using real-time data transmitted to a set of standard aircraft instruments.

Takeoff and landings were aided by dual autoland systems, which provided safe and reliable deployment and recovery under FAA Category IIIC (essentially clouds on the ground and zero visibility) conditions. The B-Gull's wide-track landing gear and speed brakes provided excellent crosswind landing capability.

The B-Gull was said to be as reliable as a manned aircraft—a feature that would be essential in a UAV that would be deployed during peacetime over densely populated areas. Equipment failure rate for the B-Gull and the man-hours required to repair such failures were estimated to be as low as 6 man-hours per 100,00 flight hours. These estimates not only mean the B-Gull would have been highly reliable, but would also have ensured low life-cycle costs. Air Force studies showed that the Compass Cope UAV was a cost-effective means of obtaining surveillance information for battlefield support, but even so, the Air Force still canceled the program.

B-Gull/YQM-94 Specifications

Length	40 ft
Wingspan	90 ft

Maximum weight	14,400 lb
Cruise speed	Mach 0.5 to 0.6
Ceiling	70,000 ft
Endurance	30 hr

TELEDYNE RYAN AERONAUTICAL
MODEL 235 R-TERN/YQM-98A COMPASS COPE

The R-Tern—Air Force designation *YQM-98A*—was the loser in an Air Force UAV competition in which Boeing's B-Gull was the winner. The R-Tern was also designed for long-endurance, high-altitude surveillance and reconnaissance missions. On its first flight, from Edwards AFB, the R-Tern climbed to 25,000 feet and reached 200 miles per hour.

The Model 235 R-Tern was designed around the basic stealth technology used in Teledyne Ryan Aeronautical's Model 154: it featured a Fiberglas flat-bottom fuselage, high aspect-ratio sailplane-type wings, and engine air intake and exhaust above the center fuselage. The R-Tern was considerably larger than the Model 154. Takeoff and landing were done on a conventional tricycle landing gear.

Mission of the R-Tern was to be strategic reconnaissance and surveillance above 70,000 feet. If the R-Tern had been selected for production, the final version would have had a different external configuration than the prototype.

R-Tern/YQM-98A Specifications

Length	38 ft
Wingspan	81 ft, 2.5 in
Wing area	347 sq ft
Maximum weight	14,310 lb
Payload for 24-hr mission	700 lb
Cruise speed	Mach 0.5
Ceiling	70,000 ft
Endurance	30 hr
Powerplant	Garrett 4,050 lb ATF3 (XF104-GA-100) turbofan

AIR FORCE ARPV (ADVANCED RPV)

The advanced RPV (FIG. 9-9) was an Air Force program in the late 1970s for a multipurpose RPV that could be used for reconnaissance, electronic warfare, and tactical strikes. Boeing, Rockwell International, and Northrop submitted proposals for the ARPV.

Each company received contracts to study a complete UAV system and build a full-scale mockup, including ground-operated controls, recovery elements, and support systems. Boeing received $646,750; Northrop, $499,614; and Rockwell International, $699,684. Objectives of the study included improved cost-effectiveness and rapid mission turnaround. The UAVs were to have retractable landing gear, internal mission-oriented bays for a variety of equipment, and low-observable characteristics.

The RPVs never made it to the operational stage because the program was canceled after the three companies' studies were submitted.

Northrop's efforts were assisted by Texas Instruments and General Research Corp. Northrop's low-cost design was based on missile designs the company had accomplished. Several mission equipment options were offered, including terrain-following equipment for low-level penetration and enhanced survivability.

The Northrop design also had a fuselage of constant section, straight wings, and an engine air intake mounted above the fuselage. It could be air- or ground-launched and had retractable landing gear.

Northrop ARPV Specifications

Length	30 ft
Wingspan	15 ft
Powerplant	GE J85 turbojet

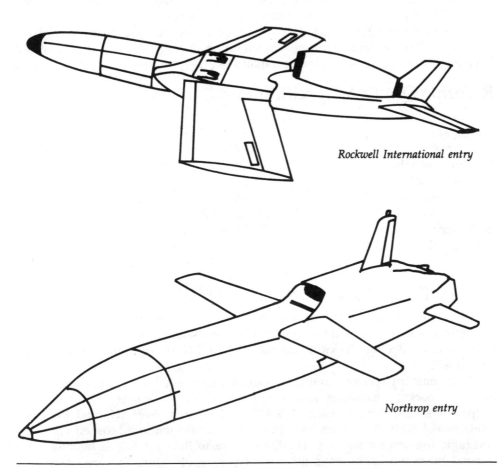

Rockwell International entry

Northrop entry

Fig. 9-9. Entries in the canceled Air Force advanced RPV program.

Rockwell's ARPV entry had slightly swept wings, a V-tail, and an engine mounted in a pod above the aft fuselage. Rockwell's ARPV also had an arresting hook for an arrested (cable-catching) landing capability.

Rockwell ARPV Specifications

Length	25 ft
Wingspan	19 ft, 4 in
Body diameter	2 ft, 9 in
Height	6 ft, 9 in

LOCKHEED MISSILES AND SPACE AQUILA/MQM-105

The Aquila is a U.S. Army UAV and is small, rugged, and cheap. It can perform a variety of missions and survive in an intensely hostile environment. Lockheed

Fig. 9-10. Lockheed/Army MQM-105 Aquila unmanned air vehicle being readied for a test mission. (Courtesy Lockheed-California)

competed against Teledyne Ryan Aeronautical's Model 272 min-RPV (based on the Benson AMR RPV-007 for the MQM-105 contract (FIG. 9-10).

The Aquila is shaped like a flying wing with a forward fuselage that is curved and blends neatly into the wing structure, with flattened wing-root extensions. The engine drives a pusher propeller that is shrouded by a circular stabilizer. The stabilizer serves the dual purpose of quieting the propeller's acoustic and infrared signatures and keeping the propeller from getting tangled in the recovery net that is used to snatch the Aquila at the end of its mission.

Automation is used to simplify Aquila's operation, allowing operators to concentrate on the mission at hand. It can be operated by qualified troops in the field, and it meets the requirements for sustained combat operations in extended battles against powerful, sophisticated enemies anywhere in the world.

A key component of the Aquila's survivability in hostile combat environments is its use of stealth technology. Its visual, acoustic, infrared, and radar signatures are almost nonexistent. Small size and careful shaping reduce its visual signature and, combined with the use of RAM, its RCS. Survival is the name of the game for any combat vehicle that is to be used successfully on a modern battlefield, and the stealth techniques used on the Aquila ensure that the vehicle will survive hostile environments and be a valuable tool for military commanders.

Airframe construction is of preimpregnated Kevlar and epoxy that is transparent to radar energy. The Aquila's RCS is so low that, during tests with the prototype, metal had to be added to the Aquila airframe so it could be tracked by radar. Many sources have stated on several occasions that, during tests, the Aquila could only be detected by radar because of the test equipment (mostly metal) it was carrying.

Modular construction is used to facilitate repair and make the Aquila easier to transport—wing panels, for instance, are removable. The vehicle is so small and light it is easy to deploy.

Although it is not a long-range UAV, the Aquila is useful at extending a battlefield commander's influence in day or night operations. When the enemy is within range of the commander's weapons, the Aquila can be used for rapid deep attacks into enemy territory. Avoidance of attacking low-value targets is made possible by effective use of the Aquila's real-time target imagery. This was one of the chief requirements for which the Aquila was designed, and it effectively provides the Army with accurate reconnaissance, target-location, target-acquisition, and laser-designation capabilities far beyond the normal range of ground observers and without risk to human pilots. The Aquila is accurate enough to permit first-round fire-and-forget, as well as the ability to adjust artillery fire by observing burst-miss distance from the target and provide immediate target damage assessment. Communications with the Aquila operator are carried out through a jam-resistant state-of-the-art electronic datalink that provides a continuous flow of information on high-value targets from the vehicle. An onboard autopilot aids in precision navigation, with position updates received from a distant tracking antenna system on the ground.

The Aquila's sensor compartment can carry interchangeable payloads weighing up to 65 pounds. An additional 35 pounds can be carried in a fuselage belly compartment.

A light Aquila system is being developed to meet the needs of the Army's rapid-deployment light forces. This UAV system is packaged in small containers that double as shelters; it can also be fitted on the Army's new HMMWV trucks, giving the UAV excellent mobility.

Aquila/MQM-105 Specifications

Length	less than 7 ft
Wingspan	less than 13 ft
Weight	260 lb
Payload (with 3 hr fuel)	60 lb
Maximum payload	95 lb

SCALED COMPOSITES CM-30

The CM-30 (FIG. 9-11) is an all-composite aircraft based on the Long EZ, an airplane originally designed by Scaled Composites President Burt Rutan for the homebuilt kitplane market. The CM-30 is built to the specifications of California Microwave, hence the "CM" designation, to fulfill a U.S. Army requirement for a UAV to perform intelligence-gathering and electronic-warfare missions under autonomous operation.

During a test in April 1987, the CM-30 flew for 13 hours under automatic control, except that the takeoff and landing was performed by a pilot who was onboard. About

Fig. 9-11. The California Microwave CM-30 unmanned air vehicle can be flown either manned or unmanned. (Courtesy California Microwave)

75 miles after taking off from Mineral Wells, Texas, the pilot switched to automatic control, then took over the controls for the landing in Marysville, California.

Two CM-30s have been built for evaluation by the Army at Ft. Huachuca, Arizona, where they will compete against another UAV design.

SCALED COMPOSITES CM-44

The CM-44 (FIG. 9-12) is a larger version of the Long EZ-based CM-30 and was also commissioned by California Microwave. Its first rollout was in March 1987.

The CM-44 is competing against two other UAVs for a U.S. Army program for a vehicle that can be flown manned or unmanned to perform battlefield reconnaissance, communication, intelligence-gathering, and electronic-warfare operations. As a manned vehicle, the CM-44 becomes more adaptable to varied mission requirements and reduces the risk to ground personnel during training and sensor-system development flights.

In addition to being built entirely of composite materials, the CM-44 has further reductions in RCS because of its flat-panel forward fuselage surfaces and top-mounted engine air intake. Its powerplant is an Avco Lycoming TIO-360 four-cylinder (probably 200 hp) piston engine driving a composite three-bladed propeller.

An aperture in the CM-44's nose is probably for some type of sensor—either laser, TV camera, or FLIR. The nose gear retracts, but the main gears are fixed, which leaves space on the center of the fuselage belly for an external pod that could carry more sensors or a jettisonable fuel tank.

Fig. 9-12. *California Microwave CM-44 unmanned air vehicle.* (Courtesy California Microwave)

CM-44 Specifications

Length	18 ft, 6 in
Wingspan	29 ft
Payload	600 lb
Cruise speed	210 mph
Endurance	18 hr

BOEING ELECTRONICS UAV

A Boeing Electronics UAV built at Boeing's Seattle, Washington, facility and rolled out in early 1986 may be related to DARPA's TEAL CAMEO PROJECT (FIG. 9-13). TEAL CAMEO is to be a tri-service UAV that comes under the jurisdiction of the DOD's and DARPA's black programs. TEAL CAMEO might be a long-endurance high-altitude successor to the Air Force's Lockheed TR-1 and the Army's Lockheed Aquila, and also the JSTARS platform. The TEAL CAMEO also could perform the now-canceled precision location strike system (PLSS) mission.

Other missions for the UAV, according to Boeing officials, could be reconnaissance; radio relay, where the UAV loiters at a high-altitude to act as sort of a satellite relay for radio transmissions; and border patrol. Boeing's UAV is a twin-engine vehicle with gull-type long-span wings and a conventional unswept empennage. The powerplants are Teledyne Continental liquid-cooled piston engines fitted with large-diameter, slow-turning, three-blade propellers that enable the UAV to fly quietly and at high altitudes. Airframe construction is of plastics that are either radar transparent, for sensor equipment bays, or radar absorbent, for the rest of the airframe. The fuselage is flat sided and has a square section with constant dimensions from front to rear. Airframe color is solid black overall.

After Boeing's UAV was constructed in Seattle, it was transported to Moses Lake, Washington, for reassembly and first flight, which took place in mid-1986. The early flights were intended to conform to design requirements. Shortly thereafter, a second vehicle joined the test program.

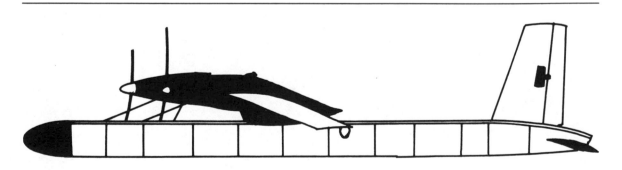

Boeing Electronics - possibly Teal Cameo

Fig. 9-13. A Boeing Electronics design that might be related to DARPA's TEAL CAMEO tri-service UAV program.

LEADING SYSTEMS AMBER

PROJECT AMBER began as a DARPA program for demonstration of a low-cost UAV with long-endurance capabilities. The AMBER UAV is a test vehicle and reportedly weighs a maximum 600 pounds. Long endurance is to be achieved through use of advanced composite structures, a lightweight engine with low specific fuel consumption, and sailplanelike aerodynamics. The UAV will use off-the-shelf payloads, which will be integrated with ground stations through datalinks. Overall control of PROJECT AMBER was to have been transferred from DARPA to the U.S. Army and Navy in 1987. The Navy planned to order 96 AMBER UAVs.

Leading Systems is the manufacturer of the AMBER UAV. The craft features a skinny fuselage that ranges from 13 to 20 feet in length and a payload volume of 5 to 15 cubic feet. The empennage is an inverted V-tail design, and a pusher propeller is mounted behind the tail. Launching can be done either from ground or ship-based facilities.

Chapter Ten

Stealth Missiles

MISSILES NEED THE CAPABILITY OF REMAINING UNDETECTED JUST AS much as aircraft.This chapter discusses five such missiles.

Missile	Status
DARPA PROJECT LORAINE	Under development
Boeing AGM-86B ALCM	Operational
General Dynamics TEAL DAWN/AGM-129A ACM	Developmental testing
Lockheed Cruise Missiles	Under development
Northrop AGM-136 Tacit Rainbow	Under development

DARPA PROJECT LORAINE

The Loraine is yet another Black Program DARPA project and is a nonnuclear, long-range, highly maneuverable missile that could be of great importance in the air-delivered cruise-missile environment of the future. The Loraine is a precision-guided, high-speed weapon that is intended for carrier battle group and continental defense missions.

The Loraine has an active sensor, called *swerve advanced radar* (SAR) that can detect and track hostile targets and guide the missile's maneuvering warhead to the target. With its high-speed capability, the Loraine missile could intercept distant enemy aircraft within a few minutes of launch. The high speed also gives the missile an extremely large search area, which reduces the need for accurate penetrating information and could allow the missile to operate without in-flight guidance updates. It is ideally suited to complement long-range surveillance/detection systems such as over-the-horizon backscatter radars or space-based infrared/millimeter-wave systems, because it can be launched at distant targets detected by these systems.

One use of these long-range detection systems is for outer-zone airspace defense of carrier battle groups. The U.S. Navy's major surface warships are now using these systems and could probably use a missile like the Loraine to complement their long-range detection systems.

In development tests of the Loraine and its phased-array SAR, the missile proved to be an excellent performer. The Loraine can be launched from the ground, from ships and submarines, from aircraft, or even from space. PROJECT LORAINE is only part of DARPA's continuing efforts in strategic bomber and cruise missile defense programs.

BOEING MILITARY AIRPLANE
AGM-86B AIR-LAUNCHED CRUISE MISSILE
AND BGM/AGM-109 TOMAHAWK CRUISE MISSILE

The AGM-86B makes such effective use of stealth technology—metal alloys and radar-transparent composites—and is so small that it is an extremely difficult target to detect and destroy (FIG. 10-1). Its engine produces a minute infrared signature, and its fuselage shape and uniquely shaped nose contribute to its low RCS. To complement its low detectability signature, the AGM-86B can fly at low levels using

Fig. 10-1. U.S. Air Force/Boeing AGM-86 air-launched cruising missile. Note the flat angled sides of the missile's fuselage and it's unique ''shark'' type nose. Both these features reduce the radar cross section of the missile, which is less than 0.5 square meters. (Courtesy Boeing Aerospace)

Tercom guidance to reduce even further the chance of being detected by enemy air defenses.

The BGM/AGM-109 Tomahawk cruise missile has similar low-observable features and a slightly different external configuration. Unlike the air-launched AGM-86B, the Tomahawk can be launched from aircraft, ships, submarines, and ground-based launchers.

Both missiles are operational. Both missiles have short-span wings that flip out after launch, although the AGM-86B's are swept slightly aft. The AGM-86B is being carried by B-52G/H bombers, but it will also be carried by the B-1B. It features a nuclear warhead—the W80-1—and is being used in the standoff nuclear strike role. The Tomahawk can carry either a conventional or nuclear warhead, depending on its mission.

AGM-86B ALCM Specifications

Length	20 ft, 9 in
Body diameter	2 ft, 0.5 in
Wingspan	12 ft
Weight	3,200 lb
Cruise speed	500 mph plus
Range	1,500 mi
Guidance	Inertial/Tercom
Powerplant	One Williams International/ Teledyne CAE F107-WR-100 turbofan, 600 lb thrust

Tomahawk Specifications

Length	20 ft
Body diameter	1 ft, 9 in
Wingspan	8 ft, 7 in
Weight	2,650 to 4,200 lb
Cruise speed	500 mph plus
Range	1,300 nmi nuclear land attack 600 nmi conventional land attack 243 nmi anti-ship
Warhead	Conventional HE or One W84 nuclear
Guidance	Land attack: inertial, Tercom DSMAC Anti-ship: strapdown attitude heading-reference system (AHRS), active-passive radar

GENERAL DYNAMICS
TEAL DAWN/AGM-129A ADVANCED CRUISE MISSILE

TEAL DAWN is an Air Force and DARPA stealth missile program begun in 1979 for an ACM to supersede Boeing's AGM-86B ALCM, in response to the threat of new Soviet air defenses.

In 1978, Lockheed flight-tested a stealth cruise missile launched from B-52 bombers flying out of Edwards AFB's North Base facility. This missile was developed in complete secrecy. When it joined the TEAL DAWN competition, Lockheed redesigned its secret stealth cruise missile in an effort to field a winning product.

Lockheed's first entry took full advantage of the company's experience with stealth technology, but the missile was aerodynamically unstable. There were also two other major drawbacks to the missile: the missile's engine had to start after the missile was ejected from the launch rack of the carrier aircraft, and the missile's unusual design (FIG. 10-2A) meant that it had to be carried externally by the carrier aircraft.

Boeing's entry in the TEAL DAWN program was a wide, flat air vehicle designed to cruise at high subsonic speeds. As can be seen in FIG. 10-2B, Boeing's ACM entry looks sort of like a shark. It was to be made of RAM, have a conformal engine air intake, and be capable of low-level penetration of enemy defenses. Boeing also proposed a modified, more advanced version of its AGM-86B ALCM.

General Dynamics proposed a variety of design concepts for the TEAL DAWN ACM program. One concept (FIG. 10-2C) featured a wrap-around horizontal stabilizer in a plane below the airframe with a vertical fin below the horizontal stabilizer to reduce RCS as viewed from above by look-down defense systems. Another concept (FIG. 10-2D) had pop-out forward-swept wings for enhanced maneuverability to enable the missile to evade SAM defenses. Other features included two small radar-transparent vertical fins, a recessed and shielded engine exhaust nozzle in the wrap-around empennage to reduce infrared signature, and a conformal ventral engine air intake.

After a fierce competition with rivals Boeing and Lockheed, General Dynamics was awarded the ACM contract in April 1983. Although the winning design is classified, it is thought to include several of the features of the two General Dynamics concepts just mentioned. (See FIG. 10-3.) It might have an oblong- or ovoid-shaped fuselage with small long-chord wings of small aspect ratio, dorsal and ventral stabilizers, small foreplanes or canards mounted on the front of the fuselage like those on the B-1B bomber, and a conformal engine air intake in the area forward of the foreplanes.

General Dynamics' winning design has one Williams International F112 turbofan engine that burns an advanced slurry type fuel. The engine was developed under the IMPROVED CRUISE MISSILE ENGINE program (ICMEP). DARPA and other DOD entities are incorporating the latest technology in the ACM, including artificial intelligence. Radar, infrared, acoustic, and visual signature reduction, and laser-reflective masking techniques will be used for low observability. The ACM will have micro-ECM and other countermeasures to help it penetrate heavily defended targets. Guidance systems will include a ring-laser gyro, Hughes forward-looking laser radar, and Tercom.

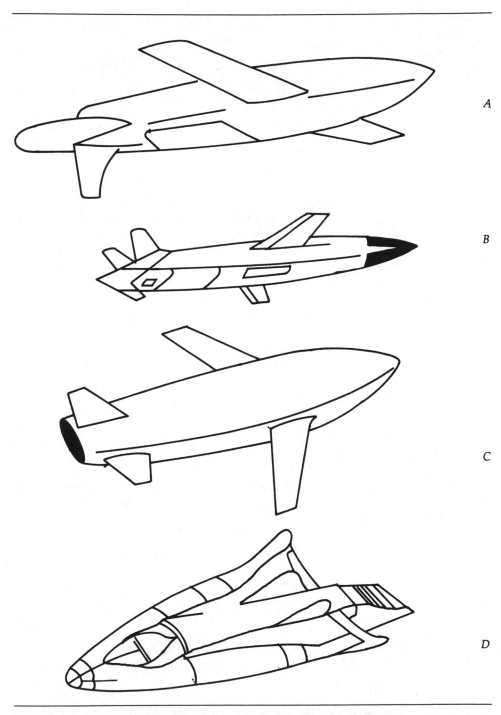

Fig. 10-2. General Dynamics advanced cruise missile designs for the Air Force TEAL DAWN *program (A,B). General Dynamics won the contract for the ACM. Boeing's proposed ACM design (C) and a lifting-body type design proposed by Lockheed for the ACM program (D) are also shown.*

Fig. 10-3. An artist's concept showing a model of the Air Force AGM-129A advanced cruise missile. (Created and photographed by Erik Simonsen.)

The General Dynamics ACM will be compatible with the common rotary weapon launcher that is to be installed on the B-52, B-1B, and B-2A bombers. First flight of the ACM was in 1984, and initial operating capability of the ACM was expected in 1987. It is possible that the ACM has already been pressed into active service in the B-1B's internal weapons bays. As many as 1,200 ACMs may eventually be bought by the U.S. Air Force for the B-1B and B-2A. In FY1986/1987, $1.2 billion was allocated for ACM production. McDonnell Douglas is second-source production partner with General Dynamics on the ACM program.

Range of the ACM should be about 3,750 miles. Its design range was specified to be 2.5 times that of the AGM-86B ALCM.

Flight tests of the ACM were delayed because of quality control problems. At least five flight tests of the AGM-129 ACM were to have been completed by June 1988. With the delay, however, the flight tests were rescheduled for fall 1988 or later.

LOCKHEED MISSILES AND SPACE STEALTH CRUISE MISSILE

The Stealth Cruise Missile (SCM), a black program advanced cruise missile being built by Lockheed for the U.S. Navy and perhaps the U.S. Air Force, has reportedly been in development since 1980. Recently the DOD confirmed its existence. The SCM's mission is to replace the Tomahawk cruise missile and be used to attack heavily defended targets such as Soviet or Warsaw Pact airfields and surface warships.

Capable of hitting within inches of a selected target, the SCM will carry conventional explosives. It is said to be a boost-glide-type missile with a range of 3,000 plus miles. The Navy recently launched an SCM from a submarine and scored a direct hit on a target 3,000 miles away. The missile can either perform attack missions or photoreconnaissance.

The successful development of the SCM, expected to take five to ten years for operational versions, will have extensive political and military implications according to DOD officials:

◇ Increasing reliance on standoff weapons that can be launched at long-distance targets, thus reducing the need for manned aircraft bombing that puts crewmen and aircraft at risk of being shot down.

◇ Reducing the loss of NATO strength that may result from a U.S.-Soviet agreement to withdraw medium-range nuclear missiles from the European theater. The SCM is so accurate that it could easily replace any medium-range missiles. The SCM also can be launched from ships, submarines, aircraft, and land-based launchers.

◇ Providing a weapon for use against terrorists. The new guidance system enables the SCM to find a target, such as a house or building, with great precision.

◇ Reducing the temptation to use nuclear weapons because an SCM with a conventional-explosives warhead could be used to achieve nearly the same result as a small nuclear weapon, with far less environmental damage and with damage concentrated only on the desired target.

A new guidance system for the SCM has been under development since 1987, as part of the CRUISE MISSILE ADVANCED GUIDANCE PROGRAM (CMAGP). This system, mounted in aircraft, was tested during the summer of 1987.

Although most of the details of the SCM and its guidance system are classified, it is known that the guidance system uses a forward-looking carbon-dioxide laser to guide the missile in the terminal phase of attack. After launch, it uses a form of Tercom and micro-INS guidance to get near the target. This technology also can be used to improve the accuracy of ICBMs and SBLMs, especially in the terminal phase when the warheads near their targets. Both General Dynamics and McDonnell Douglas are competing for the guidance system contract.

The Pentagon's Defense Science Board reviewed the SCM program and prepared recommendations to then-Secretary of Defense Caspar Weinberger urging that development of the SCM and its guidance system go forward. According to a DOD official, "Today we can fly a cruise missile through the goalposts on a football field. But if we get the new missile system, we could hit either the upright posts or the crossbar of the goalpost." The official also stated that it was too early to determine what the new missile program would cost or to estimate when it could be put into operation, although the mid-1990s were suggested as a possible timeframe.

NORTHROP TACIT RAINBOW/AGM-136A ANTIRADAR MISSILE

The TACIT RAINBOW PROGRAM began as a DARPA program in the early 1980s for an attack drone or missile for the U.S. Air Force, Navy, and Army. In November 1984, the program became a joint Air Force/Navy effort, and it was partially declassified to allow other NATO nations to participate in the development (FIG. 10-4.)

The Tacit Rainbow is intended to loiter in a battle zone, and locate and attack enemy radar emitters. The missile has a programmable guidance system using a radio-frequency terminal seeker/sensor and is armed with a conventional warhead.

Prototype Tacit Rainbow missiles were built at Northrop's Ventura, California, division, but Northrop is building facilities in Perry, Georgia, for missile production. Boeing Military Airplane, Delco Systems Operations, Singer Kearfott, and Texas Instruments are subcontractors on the program; Williams International is providing its F107 turbofan engine for the Tacit Rainbow missile.

Fig. 10-4. The very small, compact, AGM-136A TACIT RAINBOW *antiradar droning missile, seen here just before loading into the bombbay of a B-52G bomber. This is a photo of a test round.* (Courtesy Northrop)

Production of AGM-136 Tacit Rainbow was, as of August 1988, not yet started. The new missile is still undergoing developmental air and ground-launched testing. The U.S. Air Force is developing a new rotary launcher for integration into its B-52G conventional bombers. The new rotary launcher will be able to accommodate up to 30 AGM-136 Tacit Rainbow anit-radar missiles.

The missile can be air-launched by Navy attack aircraft and Air Force bombers, or it can be ground-launched from the Army multiple launcher rocker system (MLRS). There have been at least ten successful flight tests of the Tacit Rainbow, and testing continues using the B-52G, A-6E, and A-7E as launch aircraft, with full-scale development expected to be completed in FY1988.

The missile's airframe is made of radar-transparent material, and its engine air intake is positioned on top of the midfuselage. An integral solid rocket booster is mounted in the missile as well as the Williams International turbofan engine. Wingspan is 5 feet, 1 ½ inches, and the empennage is of cruciform shape, with the horizontal stabilizer mounted partway up the vertical stabilizer. Wings and empennage are folded before launch and also while the missile is in storage.

Chapter Eleven

Other Stealth Systems and Programs

STEALTH IS BEING APPLIED TO OTHER MILITARY VEHICLES BESIDES AIR-
craft. Following are some new applications of stealth technology, plus some
information on foreign stealth programs.

AIRBORNE EARLY WARNING AIRSHIP

Flying very low, virtually intermingled with the radar clutter of waves, cruise
missiles are difficult to detect and intercept. So a new way has to be developed to
counter this threat to ships at sea. Enter a proven concept with a new mission: airships.

Why airships? Because, as Melvyn Paisley, former assistant secretary of the Navy
testified before Congress, they are a ''smart, simple solution.'' From high above the
fleet with a larger rotating radar, they can look down and instantly detect and counter an incoming cruise missile. Unlike fixed or rotary wing aircraft, they can remain
on station for days, even weeks at a time, using very little fuel or other expendables.

By 1990, Westinghouse (USA)/Airships Industries (U.K.), is scheduled to build
a high-tech version of the airship, offering a low-risk, quick and cost-effective testbed platform to counter the cruise missile threat. The new airship will employ the
latest in engines, airborne electronics, and search radar technology.

Around 1960, the U.S. Navy was using Goodyear ZPG-3W airships (FIG. 11-1)
in the airborne early warning platforms against approaching aircraft. The new type
of airships would give the Navy the advange of using an existing proven design,
thus saving much time and money in development costs and minimizing development
risk.

This new airship will be faster than previous models (82 knots), more
maneuverable, and more difficult for the enemy to detect. Cruising at 5,000 to 10,000

Fig. 11-1. The configuration of Loral's AEW airship might be similar to this Goodyear Blimp, but modified for its role as an airborne long-distance radar surveillance platform. (Courtesy Goodyear)

feet, it would be capable of dropping down close to the surface to be resupplied and refueled at sea. It could stay on station 60-plus hours at a time without refueling, and indefinitely with resupplying and refueling (with a normal four-week mission period).

In June 1987, the Navy awarded a $118.2 million contract to Westinghouse/Airship Industries, for development of one airship. The contract award reflects the growing requirement for the Navy to acquire additional means of conducting antisubmarine and antiair warfare and stems from the 1983 PATROL AIRSHIP CONCEPT EVALUATION (PACE) program, which highlighted the advantages an airship would have over fixed-wing aircraft, including more time on station and greater endurance.

The contract includes full maintenance and support for the airship. In addition, another $50.7 million was allocated for the avionics suite, which will include either the APS-139 or the APS-125 radar. There is also an option for five additional airships.

First flight of the operational development model (ODM) is scheduled for late 1990, with operational suitability trails to start six months later and to continue for 18 months. The airship will be designed in Great Britain and assembly of it will be carried out at Weeksville, North Carolina, with logistics support to be provided there and at the Naval Air Station in Lakehurst, New Jersey. The Navel Air Test Center at Patuxent River, Maryland, will be the prime ODM evaluation base.

The airship will have a maximum flight speed, at stable equilibrium, of 82 knots (94.3 mph), be able to attain an altitude of 14,000 feet, and have unrefueled endurance at 40 knots (46-mph) at 5,000 feet of 60.2 hours. It will be able to .climb at a rate of 630 feet per minute, will be propelled by two 1,625-hp diesel cruise engines and one 1,750-hp turboprop sprint engine, and is to be manned by a crew of 12 to 15 people.

The operational airship, which will be more than twice of the Goodyear airship (blimp) seen on TV so often during major athletic events, will have a 30-day mission duration. A determination of the size of the proposed Navy airship fleet will not be made until at least the early 1990s, after the performance of the ODM has been extensively evaluated and tested. It has been speculated, however, that between 40 and 50 airships will be acquired by the U.S. Navy by 1995.

One problem that has not yet been publicly addressed is that, if detected, an airship makes an incredibly inviting target that would be easy to shoot down. Although it might be possible to reduce an airship's radar, acoustic, and infrared signatures to a minimum, it seems that no amount of camouflage paint will make an airship blend into the ever-changing background of sea, sky, and clouds. Also, airships are extremely slow and lack the agility that might be needed to escape enemy attackers. For these reasons, AEW airships, while useful, might be limited in their potential applications.

WARSHIPS AND SUBMARINES

The primary threat facing warships today is the antiship missile, and one such that has already earned a ruthless reputation is the French Exocet (FIG. 11-2). A more significant threat are Soviet antiship missiles that can be launched, not only by aircraft

Fig. 11-2. The French Exocet antiship missile, shown under the right wing of the French Entendard naval attack aircraft, is an extremely dangerous threat to all surface warships. This missile homes on radar signals received from the target, but if the target—such as a ship's superstructure—were made of radar-absorbent materials and other portions of the ship were painted with radar-absorbent coatings, then radar-homing antiship missiles might be less likely to hit it. Antiship missiles also home on ships that are emitting their own radar energy, so the ships might have to use alternative sensors so they do not attract these type missiles. The Soviets have an enormous number of radar- and infrared-homing antiship missiles, and thus the West does not have a monopoly on missiles like the Exocet, Harpoon, and others. (Courtesy Aerospatiale)

such as the Backfire bomber, but also from ships or submarines, or from shore installations. These missiles have been proliferating since the early 1970s, leading to explorations of ways to protect against them.

Antiship missiles track their targets using active or passive radar homing and infrared tracking. Just like stealth aircraft, ships can be coated with RAM and also use ECM/ESM in an effort to avoid being hit by an antiship missile. A ship's vulnerable superstructure can be made from RAM, provided that the materials used have acceptable ballistic-impact tolerance.

The major problem, however, is that a ship's active radar sensors make easily detectable targets for antiship missiles. All the RAM in the world will not help a ship unless new techniques are developed to keep the ship's radar sensors from providing ready targets. Military analysts have suggested that it will soon be suicidal to use active radar sensors within range of enemy weapons, and that passive infrared sensors will become the only safe sensor system.

OTHER STEALTH VEHICLES

Japan's Maritime Self Defense Force will soon commission the first known open ocean surface combatant to employ stealth technologies in their design. The stealth ships use an inverted triangular hull design, which is being applied to four destroyers currently under construction. The triangular hull shape is situated at mid and aft, with panel inclined inward seven degrees. The hull will effectively defeat radar energies from both hostile attacking aircraft, as well as antiship missiles, such as Exocet. The stealth hull design will deflect radar energy away from the ship and toward the sea surface. Further of the Aegis type in the Japanese navy also will feature this type of stealth triangular hull design.

Submarines employ a variety of countermeasures to avoid detection by ships, submarines, and antisubmarine warfare (ASW) aircraft, including quieting the submarine's engines and the propellers' noise; shaping the hull of the submarine for low detectability; using ultraquieting propulsion; using a demagnetized hull; emitting false sonar echoes to throw pursuers off track; and using a synthetic rubber coating on the hull to defeat detection systems. As a final precautionary measure, American submarines are demagnetized before they go out on patrol.

The Soviets also use a type of external submarine hull coating, dubbed *cluster guard* by NATO.

ALLIED STEALTH SYSTEMS

A number of NATO nations are interested in incorporating stealth technology in their future combat aircraft and missiles. France's Rafale, Britain's EAP, and Israel's Lavi all feature some form of stealth technology, including RAM and infrared signature reduction, but only one European manufacturer is known to be studying a pure stealth-type fighter aircraft: West Germany's Dornier. The aircraft is called the *LA-2000*, and it is reported to be a slender delta-wing design without vertical fins. The LA-2000 will fly at subsonic speeds and could be either manned or unmanned, depending on program developments.

West Germany's armed forces have a joint requirement for a low-cost, stealthy combat aircraft of this type, and IOC is specified to occur around the year 2000 or shortly thereafter.

The U.S. Air Force also has a requirement for a low-cost combat aircraft called the CAS-X, intended to replace the aging A-10. It is remotely possible that Dornier and the Air Force could codevelop the LA-2000 to fulfill the Air Force and West German requirement for a low-cost stealth fighter, but there is no evidence that this is taking place, yet.

For the Air Force requirement, one proposal has been an off-the-shelf version of the F-16 called the *A-16*, but the Air Force seems to be more interested in a new aircraft designed specifically to meet the CAS-X requirement. The new aircraft could have low detectability signatures, be highly maneuverable and agile in combat, and carry whatever weapons are needed for its missions, including a heavy-caliber internal gun system. The Air Force studied this type of aircraft a few years ago under the name BUSHWACKER, but nothing came of that project. Now, this aircraft might come back to life in the form of an Air Force version of the LA-2000.

Plessey Ltd., a British avionics firm, has produced RAM for stealth-type aircraft, ranging from narrow-band (frequency-specified) flexible plates to wide-band camouflage netting. The firm offers its services in low-observable techniques for camouflaging large structures that might easily reflect radar energy, such as ground equipment, command posts, aircraft dispersal hangars, and ships.

One RAM developed by Plessey is a honeycomb sandwiched inside Kevlar that is strong and light enough to be used as a skin for an aircraft's airframe—wings, fuselage, or control surfaces.

MIG-2000
(HYPOTHETICAL SOVIET STEALTH FIGHTER)

In the 1988 edition of the Department of Defense's booklet *Soviet Military Power*, the following was stated with concern to Soviet stealth technologies. "Signature Reduction (Stealth)—The Soviets are developing reduced-signature technologies and will be testing these technologies in aircraft and other military weapon systems. They may soon begin limited operational deployment of some 'stealth' technologies. The Soviets are believed to have built several test facilities to support their research activities."

With respect to new aircraft the Soviet might field during the next decade which might incorporate a large amount of these emerging Soviet stealth technologies, the DOD has projected two new fighter type aircraft. "To add to their growing interceptor capability, the Soviets are expected to produce two new fighters in the mid-1990s— an offensive counterair fighter, the air-superiority fighter (ASF); and a defensive counterair fighter (CAF). The maneuvering capabilities of the ASF and CAF will be significantly greater than those of the current Flanker-B (Su-27) and Fulcrum-A (MiG-29B). Initial operational capability for both aircraft, ASF and CAF, is expected in the late 1990s."

A hypothetical Soviet stealth aircraft that could be an effective answer to the U.S. Air Force's ATF by the year 2000 is shown in FIG. 11-3. The so-called *MiG-2000* already

Fig. 11-3. *Photograph of a model of another hypothetical advanced Soviet fighter, this time it is the MIG-2000. This concept has double-delta wings and forward canards. (Courtesy of Erik Simonsen)*

Fig. 11-4. *Photograph of a model of the hypothetical Soviet MIG-37 Ferret-B stealth fighter, which is being produced by the Testor model manufacturer. Model features numerous angled flat surfaces, over-wing air intakes; employed, at least in theory, to greatly reduce the overall RCS of the aircraft.*

might be on the drawing board at the MiG design center in Moscow and most probably will use some form of stealth technology.

It is known that the Soviets do have an active stealth program—the DOD has
stated that the Soviets may have developed aircraft with low-observable
characteristics—but this program is thought to be less sophisticated than American
efforts. Initial Soviet stealth efforts probably will involve adding stealth technology
to cruise missiles and manned and unmanned reconnaissance aircraft, then to combat
aircraft.

In 1987, Testor, the model aircraft manufacturer, introduced its version of a
hypothetical Soviet stealth fighter, the *MiG-37B Ferret* (FIG. 11-4). Whatever it is the
Soviets are working on—MiG 2000 or MiG 37B Ferret—there is no doubt that the U.S.
Air Force's ATF will be the most capable aircraft available to battle the latest in Soviet stealth fighter aircraft.

MiG-2000 Specifications

Length	60 ft
Wingspan	40 ft
Wing area	545 sq ft
Maximum takeoff weight	40,200 lb
Internal fuel capacity	16,000 lb
Weapons	New AAMs and an internal high-velocity gun
Internal weapons payload	3,000 lb (possibly conformal external carriage)
Powerplant	Two R-2000 turbofans with a 0.6 to 1 bypass ratio.

Augmented thrust: 27,000 lb
Normal thrust: 18,000 lb

Index